C000083980

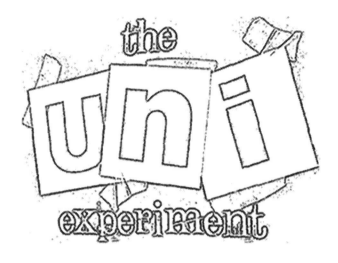

a Christian guide to the student life

tino zishiri

CHOSEN GENERATION MINISTRIES

Published by; Chosen Generation Ministries
12 Chessholme Court, Scotts Avenue, Sunbury on Thames, TW16 7ES

info@cgministries.co.uk
www.cgministries.co.uk

Cover designed by Spiffing Covers, typesetting completed by wordzworth.com and printing done by, print-and-publish.co.uk.

The website addresses recommended throughout this book are offered as a resource to you. These websites are not intended in any way to be or imply an endorsement on part of Chosen Generation Ministries, nor do we vouch for their content.

ISBN 978-0-9573595-0-5

For permission request, the author may be contacted at the following email address: info:@cgminstries.co.uk

To the student
who genuinely wants to honour God
at university

Contents

Acknowledgements

I would like to begin by thanking God for giving me the patience and strength to be able to complete my degree. I also want to thank Him for guiding me to the University of Essex, where I gained a unique experience and met unique individuals, important factors in enabling me to produce this guidebook for Christian students.

I would like to thank my family and friends, who have supported and believed in me. In particular, I want to thank my mum, whose fruits of hard labour inspire me daily. She is the reason why I work so hard. She has always supported me financially throughout my time at uni and in getting this book published.

I also want to thank a close friend of mine, Jessica Seri, for her constant encouragement. I am grateful for her support in bringing this book to reality. Having been there from the beginning, her words of wisdom and rebuke (at times painful) played a big role in making me who I am today. Lastly, I am also grateful that she agreed to do her final year research project with a view to including her findings in this book.

I am grateful for the life of Patience Bada, who has been both an inspiration and testimony of the Grace of God. She has a lot of wisdom, which I have benefited from personally - and hope that you will as well. I also want to thank her for agreeing to write a chapter for this book.

During my time at uni, I've had several spiritual figures, whose example I have looked towards. I would like to begin by thanking my Pastors at Kesed Church: Pastors Barry and Sarah Roberts. Pastor Barry has counselled me throughout my Presidency at Jesus Alive Fellowship. He gave me much-needed encouragement and advice through trying periods. I pray God's blessing over Kesed Church. Thank you both so much.

I also want to thank Reverend Thomas Yap, the then-Chaplain at Essex University. He has a distinct laugh that can be heard in the midst of a large crowd and his presence has a funny way of lightening the burdens of student life. I also want to thank him for writing a superb chapter for this book.

Special thanks go to the Proudfoot brothers. They have both been such a blessing to me. I want to begin by thanking Matt Proudfoot, founder of 'ameocreative' - what an amazing guy. He has always supported my idea and has given me so much help and guidance. He created the amazing book trailer with which you may all be familiar and has also directed me and suggested ways of moving the book forward. Thank you so much for being such a blessing, I pray God's blessings over you and your household. I would also like to thank Stef Proudfoot, founder of 'SpiffingCovers'. I want to thank him for designing the book cover with such professionalism. The concept far exceeded my expectations. I am forever grateful for your work.

I would also like to thank Kat Wiggins for her superb work with the manuscript. I want to thank her for making herself available to help me with the book, although she has so many other commitments. I appreciate her hard work and commitment.

I also want to thank David Sokan, who has been a real help in terms of designing great flyers for all the events I have been involved with; both inside and outside uni. Your efforts always exceed my expectations, thank you so much for your hard work. I appreciate you, bro.

I want to extend my thanks to the following individuals, who have kindly provided their testimonies to help inspire and encourage readers. These individuals are: Yetty Ishola, Christina Obur, Bamidele Ayilara, Tolu Salami, Jemma Greenaway, Hayley Konadu, Damy Alade, Ayo Sowemimo, Patience Bada, Jessica Seri, and Sarah Michael. Without you guys, this book wouldn't be what it is, you guys rock!

Throughout my university journey, there have been people who God has used in a unique way to add depth to both my journey and the book.

ACKNOWLEDGEMENTS

First of all, I would like to thank Kunle Oyedeji. His regular seminars have both inspired and encouraged me to realise my dreams. In particular, the Winter Wisdom Summit 2010 helped confirm my convictions for writing this book. Thank you so much for your ministry and I pray God will continue to increase it.

I want to thank Mary Osho. Although she may not realise it, God used her to provide me with an idea that I have used throughout this book. Thank you for your suggestion. I want to also thank Elwyn Latul. Thank you for being such a blessing to me and for obeying God when you did. I appreciate your help and support.

There are various groups of people to whom I would like to extend my thanks. Being at uni has meant that I have been involved in various groups, all of which have shaped me into the person I am today.

Firstly, I would like to thank my Church, Kesed, and everyone within the church. Thank you for your love and support. Additionally, I want to thank the Kesed worship team, in particular the worship leader – Matt Beales – who has continuously challenged and stretched me, not only musically, but in my character as well. I am grateful to have been part of an amazing team.

I want to the Jesus Alive Fellowship family, both past and present. Jesus Alive Fellowship has been a place where my faith has been tested and my character developed. Having had a lot of responsibility, as well as a lot of support and prayer, I am grateful for the privilege of being able to serve the society.

I am also grateful to the Chosen Generation Ministries team, both past and present. Being part of this ministry has also been both challenging and exciting. It's a privilege to be releasing this book under the ministry's name. I pray that God will continue to do great exploits through this ministry.

At this point, I would like to thank all my fellow brothers and sisters who have been instrumental to the development of my faith, character and intellect whilst at uni. In particular I would like to thank my house-mates in my first, second and third years; you know who you are!

Last, but certainly not least, I personally want to acknowledge my family back in Zimbabwe who continuously champion me. In particular, I want to thank my uncle – Simbarashe Zishiri. He is one of my biggest fans and always has something positive with which to encourage me. Thank you so much for your support, I truly appreciate it.

To those whose names I have not mentioned, God sees your effort. I thank you for having an impact in my life. Without you, this book wouldn't be what it is. Thank you all.

Note to readers

University is often painted as an experience and celebrated as such, neatly captured in the notion, "The Uni Experience". For many, this notion conjures up thoughts of freedom, fun, and money to spend! spend! spend!

Amidst all the fun and freedom, it can be easy to dismiss the important lessons of uni life as mere coincidences. For example, the fact that all of your flatmates are non-Christian may seem like a coincidence; you may even owe it to the selection process of the Department that deals with student accommodation. Thus it may be tempting to forget that you were put there for a reason, namely, "You are the light of the world" (Matthew 5 v 14).

Another example is that you may be reunited with an old friend, as many people are. It may be tempting to think, "He or she, just so happens to go to the same uni as me; well isn't that a coincidence". Unfortunately such thinking may take away the blessings that God may be bringing towards us. For some, this may be a loss in terms of a potential relationship, whilst for others it may be a loss in terms of a business opportunity.

Having made it past the first hurdle that university throws at you, i.e. getting enough UCAS points, you are sure to thrive in Higher Education. Getting past day one is another milestone and shouldn't be taken lightly. According to Introduction to Psychology, p212, "you have made a start on determining the 'goodness of fit' (Lerner, 1995) – the extent to which a person's characteristics and behaviour are compatible with the demands of a life situation."

The demands of uni life are designed to develop you as a young adult. During your time at uni, you will experience accelerated development in your faith, character and intellect, to name a few.

(The following is taken from an article titled "The development of a university student", *with my own thoughts in italics*)

The contents of the course you elected to study may change your ways of looking at the world, and have fundamental consequences for your reasoning style. *I was no exception to this, as there was a time in my life when I thought I could explain all of life using economics.*

At university, you are going to learn a lot about your work habits. Money matters may become more relevant than ever before. You might well be dealing with issues such as relocation and the impact that has on personal attachments (e.g. issues of homesickness and missing family members are very common among first-year university students). And your future role as an autonomous adult member of the workforce may loom large.

You will be an unusual student if you do not experience some heightening of anxiety and stress levels at key times (such as exams or the arrival of bank statements). Moreover, recent reports indicate that about 30 per cent of university students find themselves overwhelmed by academic demands (Montgomery & Côté, 2003).

You might change your political beliefs – or acquire political beliefs for the first time (Pascarella & Terenzini, 1991). You are likely to have to handle issues related to drugs, especially alcohol (Park, 2004), and concerning sexual activity. So, in a very real sense, at university you are living out a developmental psychology field study! *Or what I call "The Uni Experiment"*

"The Uni Experiment" is a notion I have come up with in order to encourage students to view uni life as being full of catalysts instead of coincidences.

The demands of uni life, such as handling finances and dealing with issues concerning sexual activity, are not by accident, but arise by design. We could say that the demands of uni life come about accidentally on purpose. That is, what may seem like a coincidence, is in fact a catalyst designed to accelerate the development of your faith, character and intellect.

"The Uni Experiment" stems from the fact that experiments are most commonly conducted in university laboratories. They are conducted in order to advance scientific understanding. Ironically, I have found the whole university *experience* to be an experiment in itself, a social experiment at that.

The approach of this book:

Each chapter will try to follow a similar pattern:

- Introduction
- Observation
- What would Joseph Do? (Biblical advice)
- Experiment (Practical advice)

The observations are short fictional stories that accompany each chapter. They chronicle the journey of five students who "happen" to be flatmates in Laban's court 13.1 (Also known as Lab 13.1). Unbeknownst to the students, a group of social scientists are observing them. The scientists use statistics or general observations about uni life as a hypothesis for their experiments.

The Biblical advice follows on from the situation presented in the observation. Here we look at what the Bible has to say about the specific situations.

The practical advice is given so that readers actively participate in the book and not just passively read through the material. It is hoped that, through applying the practical advice, students can maximise the advice given throughout the book.

N.B: There are some chapters where this format is not followed, due to the nature of the topic and the approach used to research the material.

PART 1

Settling In

CHAPTER 1

The fresher's arrival

The big day has finally arrived.

All summer long you have anticipated this day. I know I did.

What seemed like a far-fetched dream several months ago is now, finally, becoming real.

For many students, going to university can be accompanied by a mixture of feelings: anxiety, excitement, sadness and happiness can all be experienced as they embark this new stage of their life.

However, behind these emotions lie the various different motives for the decision to go to university. For some, it is an opportunity to improve their career prospects; others see it as the chance to meet and make friendships that will last a lifetime; some see it as an obligation to please their family and friends. It is also fair to say that the prospect of living away from home may seem daunting. Quite apart from anything else, not having the comfort of "home-cooked food" may seem unbearable for some!

The demands of university-life are different to the demands of school-life, college-life or just life in general.

Whilst at secondary school, we are treated as vulnerable individuals, who need detentions to regulate our behaviour. When we get to college, we are given more autonomy and are recognised as more mature and responsible. This is most evident in the fact that we are able to call our teachers by their first names and that detentions become a thing of the past. However, when we get to university, we are given a lot more autonomy, with minimal social or academic supervision, and the opportunity to prove to the world that we deserve to be treated like fully-competent adults.

The demands of university-life are also different from those of life in general. Unlike the outside world, university is a safer place to make mistakes; far more forgiving. For example, financial errors made at university can be cushioned by student loans, grants, bursaries, hardship funds and even student overdraft facilities, to name a few (Chapter 14), cushions and buffers that are not available in the outside world. Through trial and error, we can prepare ourselves for the outside world. However, in the same way that we shouldn't abuse God's grace, we shouldn't abuse this opportunity.

In the days leading up to freshers' week, I felt like I wasn't prepared for university, especially as a Christian. Having heard things like, "most Christians backslide when they get to uni", I was afraid that I might follow the same fate. I wish I had been handed a manual designed to help me live the student life as God intended; I would have felt more prepared and more empowered to make the right choices.

There are three main areas in which you need to prepare yourself before coming to uni, each of which relate to the three aspects of your being: you need to prepare physically, mentally and spiritually.

Preparing physically is the most obvious form of preparation, e.g. shopping, packing and making sure you have all the important documents. If you can, get your parents to do as much food shopping for you possible before going to university - they call it the bank of mum and dad for a reason! I made the mistake of not wanting to bring too much food with me, which meant I had to go to the local supermarket and compete with the other students who were in a similar position. I tell you the truth, up until that point I had never seen a supermarket that empty- you would think you had missed the rapture or something!

The second form of preparation is to do with your mindset. Do you have a strong commitment to staying on the course you elected to study? A lot of the literature that looks at why students drop out of uni, points towards a lack of preparation as a major cause (Chapter 17).

The third form of preparation, and arguably the most neglected, is spiritual preparation. The Bible contains many stories in which God calls individuals to a foreign land, usually away from family. The same individuals then find themselves in situations where their integrity and faithfulness to God are tested.

Joseph (Genesis 39) and Daniel (Daniel 1 v 8) are two striking examples. Both individuals were relativity young when God called them to a foreign land. For Joseph it was Egypt, for Daniel it was Babylon, for us it is whatever university God is calling us to.

Both individuals were tried and tested. For Joseph it came in the form of sexual temptation, for Daniel it come in the form of the temptation to defile himself with "unacceptable foods" (Daniel 1 v 8b). However, both individuals honoured God and, in turn, God honoured them. The same blessings God gave to them are also available for us as we go to university.

Observation

Prologue

A secret body of social scientists belonging to the OSE (Office for Student Experiments) has recently expanded its operations across all the universities in the UK. The OSE is a top-secret government-backed initiative. It was given a single mandate: to disprove claims that the degree was losing its value.

This came at a time when claims were being made that Higher Education institutions (HEIs) were producing a new breed of educated and unemployed young adults. The government-backed taskforce therefore sought to make the university experience more than just about getting a degree.

The organisation made use of common views about university, together with student statistics, to form hypotheses. To test the hypotheses, the scientists followed a group of students and put them through various experiments. The results from the experiments will serve to help the government better understand students. It is hoped that policies that will enhance the value of a degree will come out of this initiative. The whole process has been kept secret, so that the results are not biased.

The OSE has deployed a group of social scientists to the final university under the last phase of the initiative. After years of carrying out secretive student experiments, the organization has become adept at experimenting on students. As it is the last the ever experiment before the initiative is closed down, the organisation has called upon the pioneers of the initiative to help with the design of the experiments.

The OSE will closely follow a group of students from different backgrounds. They will examine their behaviour in order to prove or disprove the statistics and common views about the student experience. Moreover, they will be able to observe the causes that lead to the frequently quoted statistics.

Over the years, the scientists have been given limited powers by the government regarding how much they can interfere with the lives of students: they may not tamper with the environment too much, as, at the best, the experiments will yield biased results and, at worst, they may be infringing on the human rights of the students.

Each scientist has been given a guidebook, named, "Rules for monitoring", which contains a set of rules that must be followed rigidly. Among them are:

- All CCTV must be hidden from the students and must only be located in public areas (specifically, no cameras in students' rooms).
- Only audio recording is allowed in each student's room
- The scientists have control over lighting, telephone, internet and heating (with care). However, under no circumstances may they tamper with the fire alarm or anything else that may put the students' lives in danger.

Moving in

In a matter of hours, five undergraduate students from completely different backgrounds will come together under one roof; diverse people with diverse lifestyles, suddenly sharing each other's lives for the next 39 weeks. For some, this prospect brings great joy, whereas others experience anxiety.

For the most part, students are allocated their preferred accommodation and have housemates who are randomly selected. However this isn't so for the five.

Located at the largest residential development on the west of the campus, is Laban's court. It comprises 20 apartment blocks, with four floors each. If referring to the 16th flat on the fourth floor, students usually say Laban's Court 16.4. The flat designs and sizes vary; some flats accommodate four students, whereas others accommodate six. In the larger flats, there are two communal areas: a kitchen and a living room. All the bedrooms have en suite facilities.

The skies are clear and the tree branches are dancing in the breeze, whilst the sunburnt leaves have given way to the weight of the wind; it could only be autumn. After a long summer's wait, the moment has finally come. The five will finally meet.

Located towards middle of a large chain of flats, is Laban's court 13.1: an ordinary looking flat, or so it seemed from the outside…

One by one, the students enter the flat, each bringing their own motives with them:

- For Janet, it is an opportunity to break free from the parental control, a chance to embrace her independence.

- For Emmanuel, it is a chance to discover himself, as he hopes to feel part of a stable community.

- For Angela, it is an opportunity to make her dreams (or rather, her mother's dreams) come true. She arrives, escorted by her whole family, a symbol of just how proud her family is of her.

- For Kemi, going to uni is an opportunity to start again in life; new friends, new home and a new man. Her mum and dad drop her off later in the day, as her father had been preaching at their local church.

- For Chris, this is the chance to enjoy the student life. He has just come from a two week road trip in Europe. A carefree individual, he doesn't take himself very seriously.

Each flat is appointed a Residential Support Helpmate (RSH), who assists the students with any issues related to their accommodation. Thus, upon entering the flat, the students are welcomed by their RSH: Joseph. He is an international student from Israel, currently in his final year, studying Politics, Philosophy and Economics (PPE). He has dreams of returning back home after completing his degree and becoming a key political figure.

It isn't long after the students finish unpacking their belongings that they discover a large blank sheet of A2 paper with an envelope beside it. 'It's been on the table the whole time', exclaimed one of the students. In excitement, Kemi opens the envelope. She finds out that it is addressed to the occupiers of Laban's court 13.1. The letter reads as follows:

"Dear Students,

We would like to welcome you to your new home for the next 39 weeks. To help you to settle in we have provided an icebreaker to help you get to know each other. On the sheet of paper, please find space to fill in a brief personal profile, writing three things you like and three things you dislike. You may also write the course you are studying.

We hope you enjoy your stay.

Regards,

Accommodation Office"

The students are enthusiastic about the task and decide to colour the sheet of paper, including flags from their own countries. They also fill out their birthdays, but - most importantly - they fill out their likes and dislikes. They agree to add photos to the sheet of paper as the year goes on.

What Would Joseph Do?

When going to university, one of the biggest lessons you will learn is that everyone is different. Your way of doing things may be seen by others as weird and vice versa. No surprises there. However, you will also discover that all human beings are, what I like to call, "three - dimensional characters, coloured in shades of grey".

Three dimensional, in the sense that no-one is neither "all-good" nor "all-bad". Figuratively speaking, no-one is black or white, we are all grey characters. Keeping this in mind will make settling in that much easier, as you avoid making harmful assumptions about the people you will live with. In Romans 12v18, we are told 'do all that you can to live in peace with everyone'. Therefore, do your best to focus on the good side of people. Decide to have a positive expectation about people, it will help you settle in better.

Experiment

Over time, save birthday messages or cards and read over them every now and then, as – in the event of disputes - they will help you to focus on the good in people around you.

CHAPTER 2

Fresher's week

During Fresher's week, everyone is keen on meeting new people and being accepted. For some, the need to feel accepted tends to lead them to compromise their beliefs, or at least question them.

The best advice during fresher's week is simply to get involved as much as possible, within reason. Meaning, you should explore your campus and go to events that don't compromise your beliefs.

If I could count the number of times I've had a discussion, whether formally, as in a Bible study, or informally, about whether or not Christians should go raving/clubbing, I would not have enough time to finish writing this book. Personally, raving was not on my agenda when I got to uni, as I thought to myself "there are more ways of having fun than going to a rave."

I went to plenty of movie nights, free giveaways and seminars, meeting a lot of great people and this meant that I didn't feel like I was missing out on anything because I didn't go raving. Furthermore, during Fresher's week, my flatmates and I had the chance to bond really well, as we spent most of the time talking instead of recovering from hangovers.

However, to avoid sitting on the fence on this issue, I would generally advise you to avoid making a name for yourself for the wrong reasons. It can be all too easy to lose yourself at a rave and you could run the risk of being "That Girl" or "That Guy". This is especially true as a Christian: it might be that people who see you at a rave and then also see you at a Christian meeting may not take you seriously.

1 Timothy 5v24 says, 'The sins of some people are obvious, leading to certain judgement. But there are others whose sins will not be revealed until later'. Evidently, raving (which many view as a sin) is something that is obvious and not hidden. Furthermore, Romans 10 v23 -24 says, 'You say, "I am allowed to do anything" – but not everything is good for you. You say, "I am allowed to do anything" – but not everything is beneficial. Don't be concerned for you own good but for the good of others". In view of the above, we observe that what you do will have an effect on others around you, especially if it is clearly visible. As such, Christianity is not just about you, it's about other people as well; you have to think about how going to a rave will affect other people, both Christians and non-Christians.

During Fresher's week, everyone is your friend, but it is quite possible that the people you hang around with during Fresher's week could simply become "hi-bye friends" by the time you graduate.

Observation

Hypothesis: Binge drinking has become a large part of fresher's week.
According to a group of experts, "Fresher's week" has been transformed from an opportunity for students to get to know each other, familiarise themselves with their surroundings and join societies, into an alcoholic haze in which memories are lost, ditches fallen into and drink-related accidents reign.

Ring of fire

Midway through Fresher's week and the students start to familiarise themselves with their surroundings. In particular, the girls have decided to go around the campus together and explore, making friends along the way. Keen on not being left out, Emmanuel joins them, whilst the other guys remain in their rooms.

It doesn't take long until one of the students decides to make their university experience a bit more interesting. In the evening, Chris invites a few of his new friends over to the flat. Unaware of this, the other students, who are currently in the kitchen, are engaged in a deep conversation about how social media is changing the world.

Whilst in the middle of hearing Emmanuel's point of view, Kemi, Janet and Angela hear a loud knock on the front door. This is shortly followed by "don't worry guys, I'll get it", as Chris quickly comes out of his room to open the door for his guests. Before opening the door, he quickly explains to his on looking flatmates that he has invited a few friends to play a game "with a bit of twist".

One by one the guests start coming into the flat, three in total. After a few introductions, the kitchen suddenly becomes quiet as all eyes turn on Chris. Aware of this, he quickly explains to everyone how the night is going to go, telling them that they are going to play "Ring of Fire", a game which everyone in the kitchen - apart from his housemates – already knows how to play.

Chris explains the rules of the game, "First I will put a cup in the middle of a deck of cards arranged in a circle. Each person will then get a cup filled with lot of coke and a bit of twist. One person starts by picking up a card and, whatever the card may be, following the rule. The game proceeds in a circle and everyone picks a card until the last card has been picked. However, before we start the game, all of you must know what each card stands for." Chris goes on to explain what each card stands for, e.g. A = Waterfall (meaning everyone must drink until the person that picked the card stops drinking, 8 = Mate (meaning choose someone to drink with you).

"So what is the twist?" asks Emmanuel. Chris replies "I thought you would have figured it out by now, the twist is JD...as in Jack Daniel's. We are going to have JD and Coke". Immediately Emmanuel's heart starts racing; he has never been drunk before, although perhaps a little tipsy on one occasion. He is left in the middle of a moral dilemma.

Conversely, Angela immediately declares herself out, "I am not involved", she says, as she takes her faith into account.

Kemi, is in a similar position to Emmanuel, she too is met with a moral dilemma. "This is not something that my dad would be proud of", she utters to herself. However she then reasons, "then again, has he ever taken pride in anything I do?" Being a pastor's child has often left Kemi feeling like she is never good enough to meet her father's high standards. In the end, Kemi decides to participate.

The decision to play the game was as easy for Janet as the decision to go to a uni as far away from home as possible. "It's only a bit of fun. Besides, it's not like there is any parental control stopping us", says Janet. She then declares herself in. Not wishing for anyone to be left out, she tries to persuade Angela to join. However Angela is adamant not to get drunk, as she doesn't want to set a bad example.

Chris finally finds a compromise solution, suggesting that Angela can just drink Coke without the JD. In the midst of all this, Emmanuel has remained quiet, fiercely calculating the costs and benefits involved. He thinks to himself, "If I don't join the game, I will be labelled as a religious party pooper". However he doesn't want to get drunk. Hence, when Chris suggests the compromise solution, Emmanuel immediately smiles and quickly agrees to participate on those terms.

At the end of the game, Chris, Kemi, and Janet, along with the three guests, have got very drunk. Unfortunately for one of Chris' guests, it was their first time getting drunk and she ended up not feeling very well, unaware of just how much alcohol she could handle.

The students have confirmed the scientists' hypothesis. However Emmanuel and Angela have deviated from it. After observing the drinking game, a debate starts to develop among the scientists. Some say it's the new found freedom that causes the students to get involved in drinking culture, using Janet as an example. However others say that it is down to peer pressure. Their main argument is supported by the fact that for one of the guests it was their first time getting drunk.

What would Joseph do?

In a report by the Christianity and the University Experience (CUE) project "Of the Christian students surveyed, just fewer than 65% are against or have some problem with the drinking culture that they encounter at university, compared with 54% of non-Christians".

This leaves around 35% of Christian student surveyed, who did not have a problem with the drinking culture at university. In view of this, it comes as no surprise that Christians can find themselves immersed in the drinking culture of today.

It's important to start uni the way you intend to continue, in order to avoid being labelled as a Christian who is "not serious" about their faith. Try getting involved in as many activities as possible, but avoid doing what you wouldn't do at home. Although this is much easier said than done, it will work out best for you in the long run.

Experiment

- Find ways of having fun without compromising on Christian values.
- Make it your duty to find other followers of Christians during Fresher's week.

CHAPTER 3

Homesickness

In response to the question "What, if anything, do you consider to be the best aspects of university life?" 34% of the respondents said "moving away from home". For many, the freedom gained from uni-life is part of what makes it so attractive. This could be for a number of reasons, e.g. pressures back at home, or unrest within the family, and can explain why some students may choose to remain at uni instead of going home during the holiday period.

While there are many reasons to stay away from home, it is important to remind yourself of where you will return at the end of your degree - on average, the student life is only three years. It is also important to remind yourself that you will need something that says, "this is what I did with my three years at uni". Such realisations can help you keep focused, although this isn't guaranteed. Ultimately whether you bring home a 2:1 or a 3rd is up to you.

Experiencing homesickness at uni, during the first few days or even weeks, is not uncommon. In response to the question "What, if anything, do you consider to be the worst aspects of university life?" 13% of respondents said "Homesickness". Missing home may lead to a lack of social integration which is listed as one of the main reason why some students drop out.

One of the most influential theories surrounding student dropouts is the Tinto Model outlined by Draper (2006). The model suggests that a student's social and academic integration into uni is important if students are going to complete their degree. For now, we shall focus on social integration. In chapter 17, together with other reasons, we shall look at the role academic integration plays in ensuring that students complete their degree.

Social integration is simply how well you fit in with the people around you. During your first year, you will be living with people you have never met before. Different lifestyles will all come under one roof and social integration will be important, as you will be living with each other for the next 39 weeks or so.

According to Draper (2006), family background is a key influence on integration and thus degree completion. This is because it is likely to influence "preparedness for and commitment to" university. Coming from a single parent background, I went to uni with the view to eventually support my family. As stated above, I had to show something for my three years spent at uni.

That said, nothing could have ever prepared me for the times when people on floor above would keep me awake until 6am in the morning, after having gone upstairs twice to tell them to keep the noise down. However, you should keep focused on the bigger picture.

Testimonies

Yetty, BA Politics and sociology

Coming to university is meant to be one of the happiest times of your life, a time to meet new people and experience new things. When I arrived I was all ready to go out and make the most of my university experience and that is exactly what I did. At first, I was a bit nervous coming to a new place and not knowing anyone, but after my first night I started making friends.

As the term went on, I had joined a few clubs and had made quite a few friends. I spent a lot of my time with people just having fun; I hardly spent any time in my room, but I was in everyone else's room or going to Jesus Alive Fellowship, a Christian society. Even though I was having fun, I always felt alone; as though no-one knew the real me.

When it came to the end of term, I had convinced myself that I didn't belong at Essex University, that this feeling of being alone was more than home sickness. So, when I went home for Christmas, I decided that I was not going to come back to Essex, although I didn't tell anyone at University what I was planning. However, when I got home, I realised I had to tell my mum and dad that I wanted to drop out of university and I didn't know how that would go, so I put off telling them for a while.

By the end of my Christmas break, I had changed my mind and, feeling like it was more God than me, decided to go back to university and see how things went. On coming back to university, I gave a testimony in JAF about how I had been feeling and my plans. As I was giving my testimony, I remember the shock on one of my friend's faces, like she couldn't believe that we had spent time together and yet I never shared any of this with her. After I gave that testimony, I felt like I could move on in life and I am so happy I never dropped out, because I know now that God brought me to this university for a purpose beyond just a degree and I also thank Him for helping me prosper in my studies.

Observation

Hypothesis: Christians may be more likely to get homesick than their non-Christian flatmates; the scientists reckon that Christians are more likely to get homesick within the first few days of moving to uni than non-believers, especially if they are coming from a strong Christian family.

The morning after the night before

Upon waking up after the previous night, Angela immediately starts reflecting on the previous night. Although she didn't drink any alcohol, let alone get drunk, she feels that it's not something of which her parents would approve. She murmurs to herself "what sort of example am I setting?"

It's not long before Angela starts missing her family, especially the devotion time she used to have with them. Her whole family would meet in the living room, to share the word and pray for each other. In an effort to relive past memories, she calls her mum.

It isn't until she has been speaking on the phone for an hour, that she realises that she is homesick. This is worsened by her fear of not finding a new church where she can grow spiritually and have a clearly defined role within it.

Whilst Angela is on the phone, Janet wakes up with a throbbing head-ache. Thoughts of regret are immediate, as she questions herself, "why did I get so drunk?" After finding the strength to get up, she goes to the kitchen and sees what a mess they left it in after last night.

Janet responds badly to jokes that suggest that women belong in the kitchen. Growing up, she has never liked the image of females doing all the kitchen work. However, to her surprise, she doesn't know what's worse, conforming to that image or the state of the kitchen.

Concluding that the kitchen is too messy for her liking; she decides to swallow her pride and clean up. However, she is determined to call a house-meeting, as she feels that all her other housemates have left her to do the kitchen work, as if to purposefully annoy her.

As soon as Janet starts cleaning up, Angela comes from her room into the kitchen.

"Oh wow, this is messy", says Angela. With a hint of sarcasm, Janet replies "You're telling me", adding, "to be honest with you, if this is what I am going to have to put up with for the next 39 weeks, then uni is not for me."

Angela replies, "I can understand where you are coming from. I felt like going back home earlier, but leaving uni is a bit much, don't you think?"

In the end the girls agree to look out for each other. They have both found that being away from family and home comforts can make the initial stages of uni-life overwhelming.

What would Joseph do?

It can often be hard to identify other Christians during Fresher's week. Your housemates are probably not going to be Christian themselves and you may feel as if you are the only Christian there. You will also need to find a new Church. All of this can lead you to miss home, where you had a clear role and routine.

The Bible, in Psalms 68 v6a, says 'God places the lonely in families'. I believe that it is talking about a family of believers. There will be times where you feel isolated from other brothers and sisters in Christ and this is especially true at the beginning of your student life.

You may make numerous friendships at the beginning of your journey as a student. Although such friendships will meet your social needs, as it's not good that man should be alone, such friendships may fail to meet your spiritual needs, as the people you initially meet may not be followers of Christ. Only by surrounding yourself with fellow Christians will you find yourself able to relate at a deeper level.

This begs the question, 'Is it wrong for me to befriend unbelievers?' My response to this is a resounding 'no'. Having unsaved friends gives you the opportunity to witness to them with your life. Having only saved friends will meet your spiritual needs as well as your social needs, but will put a limit on the level of impact we Christians have on campus.

Experiment

Try as best as you can to keep in touch with friends you have left at home.

The best way to avoid homesickness is to fellowship with other believers and form a strong family culture. Being part of a Christian fellowship is a source of tremendous help and support. In particular, when you are weak, you are guaranteed to find people who are strong, and vice versa. In the absence of such a strong network of support, the demands of uni life can become unbearable and the subsequent inability to cope with the pressures of university life has been identified as a reason for why many students drop out of uni.

More than anything, it's important to get rooted into a local church were you able to grow spiritually and also serve. Try visiting as many churches as you can within the first few weeks of being at uni. It may take a while at first, but once you've found the right place you will be glad for having searched. Other students, especially those within Christian societies, can also offer help in your pursuit of a church.

CHAPTER 4

Friendships

A big attraction of going to university is the opportunity to meet new friends. In the Student Experience report 2007 by UNITE (provider of student accommodation), in response to the question, "What, if anything, do you consider the best aspects of university life", meeting new friends came joint first, with 59% of the respondents stating that it was as important as improving career prospects.

During Fresher's week, and sometimes even a few weeks into uni, it's possible that student may not fully identify themselves as belonging to a particular group – it can be hard to find to find like-minded people. However, you may be fortunate enough to have the right kind of housemates or for an appropriate society to be hosting an event during Fresher's week. It is more likely that you will meet the right kind of people at Fresher's fair.

In a report by the UNITE Group, it was stated that "more than one in three (35%) ex-students have trotted the globe because of uni friends or contacts. In contrast, 78% of non-students feel they have missed out on once in a lifetime experiences abroad due to not going to university."

I had the privilege of going away on a weekend break in Malta with a few close friends. Weeks of planning and last minute changes, culminated in a weekend to remember. At only around £110, the trip was well within our student budget, especially as we had just got our student loan. After what was a crazy start (almost missing the flight), we arrived in Malta ready to enjoy some fun, freedom and exploration. The trip gave us all a chance to see each other in a different environment, namely away from uni.

Intent on exploring the city, even at the risk of getting lost, we allowed the wind to take us where-ever it pleased. For some, though, this was quite literal and – unfortunately - they ended up so lost that we concluded that there must have been some form of divine intervention that rearranged the roads in such a way that one could end up as far right as possible after having taken a left turn. That said, in their defence I would like to point to the adage, "two wrongs don't make a right: but three lefts do." Adventures aside, what was particularly important about the experience was that, amidst all the fantastic kebabs, fancy restaurants, horse and carriage rides and bus tours, we still had time to hold a Bible study.

Aside from potential trips abroad, the people that you stay with are crucial to your social well-being at uni. It is common practice among universities to offer guaranteed halls of residency accommodation to all first years. As wonderful as this may be, it doesn't guarantee that you will get equally wonderful house mates. I was blessed enough to have really good flatmates in my first year. If this is not the case for you, make sure you choose your housemates for next year carefully.

What to look for in potential housemates

- Ideally, try to move in with fellow Christians. This will avoid the problems that may arise when you live with non-Christians, for example if you wish to host Bible study in your room.

- Ideally, try to move in with people of the same sex. This is especially important for guys, as many lack authentic male relationships, especially with Christians. Moving in with the guys in both my second and final year was one of the best decisions I've made at uni. It will pay off in more ways that you will realise.

- Ideally, try to move in with people you will be comfortable living with for at least a year. Moving in with friends is an obvious decision. But even if you are not familiar with the person, get to know them months before deciding to move in with them. This will help avoid problems down the line.

- Most of all, ask for God's direction over the decision. Ultimately, He knows what will work best for you in this area.

Observation

Hypothesis: Friendships formed at uni are more likely to be stronger than those formed outside uni. The UNITE Group stated that, "friendships forged at university are [...] more likely to be closer than those formed at school or work." More specifically, "on average, people who go to university end up with 15 very close friends, compared to just 10 for those who choose not to do a degree."

A sense of belonging

It's Fresher's fair and each student is excited about meeting people who share the same passions and views. In particular, Angela is hoping to meet like-minded people who share the same faith as her. She is also keen on joining the law society, even though she isn't studying law.

Emmanuel joins the law society and the same Christian society as Angela. He joins the law society, because he believes that it will help him with his degree and the Christian society, as he has decided to take his faith more seriously, even at uni.

Joseph, along with being a Residential Support Helpmate, is on the executive team for the PPE society. He is also a member of the Christian society, where he is one of the Bible study leaders.

Kemi and Janet love their r 'n'b, so they both decide to join the r 'n'b society. However, when it comes to joining sport clubs, they have completely different goal and motives. On the one hand, Janet joins the women's football club, as football is her passion, while Kemi joins the cheerleading club, after finding out that a guy who lives upstairs from her is part of the men's basketball team. She hopes to grab his attention before and after games.

Chris has chosen to join as many societies as his curiosity will allow him. He ends up joining half a dozen societies, costing him more than he had hoped. The variety of his choices seems to reflect his eclectic tastes, ranging from the debating society to the Skiing society.

A few weeks into uni, identities become more and more cemented, as people become more associated with their societies and groups. This fact becomes true of the six housemates living at Laban's court 13.1. Through the Christian society, Angela, Emmanuel and Joseph become closer and regularly encourage each other.

Similarly, through the r'n'b society, Kemi and Janet are soon using each other's iPod, sharing unity in their similar musical tastes.

Despite belonging to different societies and having different beliefs, the students' friendships seem to strengthen as time goes by. Although they have had few disagreements over noise levels and the issue of plates being left unwashed, they generally get along.

After observing the process by which the students have formed their friendships, the scientists try to understand why such friendships are stronger than those formed outside uni. The scientists have identified two reasons:

- The students have befriended like-minded people, which is easier to do at uni than any other environment, given the number of societies and clubs available at Fresher's fair.

- The students are in constant contact. By living together, the six housemates are like a family, sharing each other's lives. Building intimacy and trust is easier if you see the other person every day.

What would Joseph do?

In view of the above, it is important to bear in mind the following three facts about friendships.

1   Not all the friends you will make at uni will be Christians.
2   Not all Christians will be your friends (a sad realisation, perhaps).
3   Some of your friends may be backslidden Christians.

Fact one

Being the Chosen generation that we are, it is important to win souls for Christ. However this will be difficult if all your friends are Christian. Having non-Christian friends gives you the opportunity to influence them for Christ. God gave me this opportunity in my 1st year of uni and, as a result, I was able help someone learn things that even I myself didn't know - I sincerely believe that God spoke through me. Afterwards I was told by the individual concerned that they still think about those things and will probably do so forever. (Personal Evangelism, chapter 10)

Fact two

A great misconception among young Christians is that everyone within the Kingdom of God is supposed to be your best friend. Unfortunately, this is not the case and often far from it! It is important to know that unity is vital within the body of Christ, but we must understand that a sincere real friendship with another person requires a lot of effort. God has created everyone differently; everyone has their likes and dislikes. Some people we meet, we click with instantly, but with others it's a different story!

The real problem is when we then belittle one another. Honouring each other, despite the differences, is a skill Christians have to adopt. Ever heard the saying, "you can only fail if you try to please everyone"? The same applies in the Kingdom of God. We often put such value on the opinions of others that we develop into 'people pleasers', putting people before God. It is important to understand that not everyone around you will necessarily like you or want to be your friend. Get over it and move on!

From the life of Jesus we can see that, minutes away from His divine destiny at the cross, his so-called friends had forsaken him. At times, the closer you are to your divine destiny, the more alone you become.

Fact three

Amongst our group of friends, it is most likely that some will be backslidden Christians. It is easy to respond by judging them; however a better response would be to show compassion. There will be times in your life where you will feel superior to someone, thinking "at least I am not doing that." However there will be times when you will find yourself in the opposite situation. This can be a very humbling process, allowing you to appreciate what the other person is going through.

However, there is also a difference between confessing your sins and showing off your sins. You can hear the person's problems and pray for them, you can even advise them to get a mentor, but if that person starts disrespecting you, having no shame and showing off their sin as if to tempt you, you should rebuke them. Although you should restore gently (Galatians 6v1), you should make sure that you don't fall into the same temptation yourself.

Experiment

- Choose your future housemates from people that go to the same societies as you
- Join a society that will strengthen your views and values.

PART 2

Academics

CHAPTER 5

Myths about academic success

Since first year doesn't count, I can get away with just a pass

It is true that for many undergraduate courses, the first year of university doesn't usually count. In a 3 year course, it may be that only the penultimate and final year counts. Thus, it may be tempting to put in minimum effort and get away with barely passing. For individuals that adopt this mindset, other things like the social life and sleep may seem more pressing. Such individuals tend to claim that "I'll get serious when the second year comes".

Personally, I believe that this mindset is self-limiting; it limits the amount of opportunities available to you. For those hoping to go into the corporate world upon graduation, or any profession for that matter, the phrase "what matters is not what you know, but who you know" comes to mind. Graduating with a first class degree is a tremendous advantage when entering into the job market, but it doesn't guarantee immediate employment, given the competition. Equally important, if not more in some cases, is some form of work experience. This tells the employer that you are not just about the theory, but you are also practical. However, the most important factor in finding a job after graduation is having contacts.

Contacts within an organisation or field are best positioned to help you secure a job, especially if you are in good standing with them. The best way to get contacts, in my opinion, is through internships and work experience.

It is becoming a norm to offer internships to students in their penultimate year of study and one striking thing about the internships on offer is the predicted grades they require. In my experience, most organisations ask that applicants be on track for a 2:1 as a minimum requirement.

Assuming that you are applying for summer internships, applications typically begin at the start of September and carry on until March or April. So, it should be fairly self-explanatory why it is advantageous to be getting a first in your first year at university.

The exam season is stressful

Claiming that this is a myth may be slightly controversial, given that we all experience some degree of stress during the exam season. However, I believe that this doesn't necessarily have to be the case. In preparing for my final exams in my second year of uni, I truly experienced the peace of God during that season.

I had an assurance within my spirit that God had already done it for me and that all I needed to do was put my faith into action - after all faith without works is dead. I had so much faith and had put in a lot of work over the course of the year, so that I was even able to take a break where I did no revision. Instead, I spent a weekend away at a two day Church conference where my spirit was radically lifted. This was after I had written five exams and was three days before my last exam.

The peace grew so strong that, a few hours before my last exam, I had reached the stage where I felt like I had finished revising. When my friends saw me, they commented "you don't look like someone who has an exam in a few hours" or something to that effect, and it was true: the peace of God had given me so much assurance that even my friends took notice. You could say that it surpassed our own understanding.

I can get away with last-minute revision

On a spirit level, the peace of God was the main factor that helped me to stay stress-free for most of the exam season, but I would be lying if I was to say I didn't have any anxious moments. On a practical level, what helped to stay stress-free was starting my revision early. It is for this reason that I believe that last minute revision is never a good idea.

Last minute revision induces unnecessary stress, which could be avoided by simply starting earlier. Suppose in your final exam you have between four and eight exams and suppose that you want to spend at least 25 hours revising for each exam, we can assume that 150 hours will go towards revision.

Table 1. *Breakdown of study hours towards exams*

Weeks before exams	Weekly hours	Daily hours
6	25	3hrs 30mins
5	30	4hrs 15mins
4	37.5	5hrs 20mins
3	50	7hrs 10mins
2	75	10hrs 40mins
1	150	21hrs 25mins

As this table shows, the sooner you start revising; the fewer hours you will have to do each day. As a result, you can afford to take a break, within reason, and still achieve to the best of your ability. This idea worked really well for me.

After the exam season quite a few people around me remarked at how stressful the exam season had been. For them, they were glad that it was finally over. For me, however, in a testimony I gave, I confessed how I didn't feel like the exam season had finished as I didn't feel like it had started. I didn't overburden myself with the stress of last-minute revision; instead I started earlier and had the peace of God working in me.

You have to be really clever to get a first

I believe that this is a myth because what you lack in one area, you can usually make up in another area. In my case, if cleverness was measured by how good your memory is, I would have to start my revision incredibly early to make up for the shortcomings in my memory.

I sincerely believe that anyone can attain a first if they have faith with works. Having faith in God will help you believe in yourself and believing in yourself is a good motivation when it comes to the exam season. Believing in yourself is also a good attitude to have generally and can be more advantageous than having natural aptitude or intelligence, as we shall soon discover.

Cutting back on God-time will help you get more work done

During the first term of my second year of uni, I had been given a role within the Christian society of which I was part. Although challenging, my role forced me to discipline myself. I had to wake up very early every Monday and Friday to make sure I was on campus by 8am, to either lead or help lead the prayer meetings.

Although it appeared that I was putting God first, the reality was, I had other things that were taking priority in my life. From the little that I know of God, He will always expose any form of idolatry because He is a jealous God (Exodus 20 v 5).

This manifested itself in the form of a low mark in an assignment. At this point I would like to say that there is no disappointment without purpose when you are in the will of God. The purpose could be a lesson for you and others to learn from.

After having worked closely on an assignment with a few friends, the time came to hand it in. I was confident that I had got a first, since one of the "clever guys" I had worked with had showed me how to solve the most difficult question on the assignment.

On the day the results came back, I asked my friend Jessica if she collected her results. "Yeah I did, I got 73%", was her reply. My response was a mixture of confusion and frustration, as I had only got 62%. It didn't make sense to me, as our solutions were more or less identical, because we had worked closely with other people.

It was then that I realised that God was teaching me a lesson. I thought to myself, "maybe I should go and get it remarked", but I didn't bother. Instead, I tried to find the lesson behind it. I realised that I wasn't putting God first. Passion for God's house didn't consume me, as it should (Psalms 69 v 9).

When I eventually I took my paper to get it remarked, I ended up with 75%. My teacher had missed out 13 marks; I believe that, those 13 marks started something that has been stirring up inside of me for some time. Namely, "seek the Kingdom of God, above all else, and live righteously, and he will give you everything you need".

I decided that I was going to become more passionate for God's house in my second term. That decision came at the same time that my local church (Kesed) was looking for a bass player to join the worship team. If you ever get a chance to visit Colchester, and if it is a Sunday, I encourage you to go there; the atmosphere in that church is phenomenal. Joining the worship team pushed me out of my comfort zone and made more room for God's grace.

With less time on my hands and new responsibility alongside my existing responsibilities, I started to use my time more wisely. I had a sense of urgency when it came to my studies. In the next chapter "Attitude and Aptitude" well shall look at some of the things I changed.

In the end, I ended up getting a higher mark in my second term than in my first term and I truly believe that this was because I chose to put God first. As a result, I don't believe that forsaking God in order to get more work done, is beneficial.

God will do the work for me

I believe that God wants us to prosper in every area of our lives, academia being no exception. That said, I also believe that God works with you not for you. God cannot remind you of a formula that you have never seen before!

In the same way that make-up can enhance the beauty of a woman, I believe God enhances the knowledge that we already have. This can be done either through calling it to remembrance or helping us to make connections between information. However, you have to give God something to work with.

It can also be tempting to think, "because I am being passionate for God's house, I can get away with mediocre work, and still do well." However, "faith without works is dead" (James 2 v 26). This is another lesson that I learnt: I thought because I was so involved with God's work, that He would do my work and, as a result, I ended up get 54% in one of my assignments.

CHAPTER 6

Attitude and Aptitude

I believe that academic success depends on your attitude as much as it does on your aptitude. There is more to academic success than just natural intelligence, especially at this level. A degree requires deadlines to be met, motivation to study alone, and the wisdom to achieve a healthy work–life balance, to name a few. Try and make a list of all the factors that you think lead to a good grade and then categorize the factors into either attitude or aptitude.

Below are a few thoughts to help us get started:

- Attitude is how you view your degree. Aptitude is how you complete your degree.

- Attitude says I have got a first class already. Aptitude is doing the right things to maintain that level.

- Attitude is to do with the mind. Aptitude is to do with the brain.

Attitude

Definition: The way a person views something or tends to behave towards it.

Attitude plays a very big part in your final result. The greatest thing about it is that it doesn't take a genius to have a positive attitude towards studying. It doesn't require too much effort to develop a positive attitude; it all starts with a single thought.

Given its potential and how easy it is to develop, changing how you view your degree is essential. I am confident that your output will be greater than your input.

View your degree as a job

Have you ever had a job? If so, how many hours did you usually work each day? University serves to prepare students for the real world. Most students are likely to end up in a "9-5, 5 days a week" type of job. Since this is going to be the case, why not prepare for the real world, by viewing your degree as a job?

I used to be surprised that I found it easier to work for six hours than to study for the same amount of time. However, learning to view my degree as a job, lead me to conclude that, if I can spend six hours working, then I can definitely spend at least six hours studying.

Working for six hours may seem easier than studying for six hours simply because a job provides an immediate financial reward, whereas the rewards of studying are more distant.

Training yourself to view your degree as a job will help you in the present as well as the future. In the present, it can help you stay on top of the workload. In the future, when you step into the real world, you will have trained yourself to be able to work that long.

Working smart

Text books may not be very useful in explaining every theory and this may prove to be frustrating, cause you to go into autopilot, reading and rereading the material, desperately trying to take in the information. Maybe one or two hours into it, you may conclude that you've done a lot of work. However this doesn't guarantee that you have understood any of the material.

Going to the office hours of academic staff in your department allows you to get help on a one-to-one basis, so that every question or confusion that you may have can be cleared up.

Office hours also saves you time, because you may be able to clarify what the examiner expects from students. It may be that certain skills need to be demonstrated in a particular exam. From previous experience, lecturers and professors are usually impressed by such a display of determination. So make it work to your advantage.

And it can be a tremendous advantage, as the person setting the exam is likely to be the lecturer or professor you may be going to see. This is unlike secondary or further education, where the exams are set by examining boards. Although exams are marked anonymously, using office hours for the above mentioned reasons gives you a great advantage above your peers. Again this doesn't take a genius to figure this out.

Develop a sense of urgency

At the start of term, exams and coursework may seem so far away that it can be tempting to get complacent. However, a sense of urgency is needed to help you keep on top of the workload and deadlines. Make sure you always compare your progress to a syllabus and never to other people.

Here is a thought: having a sense of urgency can turn a book into a chapter and a chapter into a paragraph, and a paragraph into a sentence, until words become letters. This is a very big advantage. It allows for active learning, rather than passively taking information in.

When writing notes, you don't have to copy down everything. Remember, in the end, your performance in the exam is more down to how much your brain processed and understood than how many pages of notes you wrote down.

Use shorthand to turn a "word into a letter", learn the rule and apply it every time it's applicable. This will help you be alert as you start to actively take in the information. This is more effective if you create your own shortcuts. The key to doing this is to make a list of the most common phrases or words.

As a student of economics a common word that comes up is "value". Thus, when making notes, I tend to write V_{AL} instead of "value". The most important thing is that you make it personal to yourself. This requires some level of thought and creativity, however once explored, it will worth it in the amount of time it save.

Using shorthand to turn a word like solution, into sol$^{\underline{n}}$ or equilibrium into eq$^{\underline{bm}}$ will help to save time when making notes. A key to this kind of shorthand would be to find innovative ways to turn common suffixes like "*tion" or "*ship" into symbols or shorthand.

Below are a few techniques that I've picked up that have helped me turn a "word into a letter", so to speak.

Table 2.   *Symbols and shorthand*

Word	Symbol/Shorthand
Advantage	↑ (Coloured green)
Disadvantage	↓ (Coloured red)
Imply	→
Therefore	∴
Better than	>
Change/Difference	Δ
Equals not	≠

Word	Symbol/Shorthand
Positive	$+tve$
Negative	$-tve$
Relationship/link	$\leftrightarrows$

Active learning is where you begin to notice themes within texts, so that you are able to identify similarities and differences. You will compare new information with previous information stored in your brain. Once you get to this stage, you will begin to see the bigger picture and are likely to enhance your performance.

A sense of urgency will really help you focus on the "crucial 20%" (read below).

There will be times when your course will seem uninteresting and, as a result, you may lose your sense of urgency. However what I always do to overcome this problem is to find current information on my subject through newspapers, the internet and the TV among other things. This helps to make my course more interesting and relevant.

80/20 rule - Pareto efficiency rule

The rule/observation states that: For many events, roughly 80% of the effects come from 20% of the causes. In other words, 80% of your results come from the crucial 20% of the things you do.

The original observation was in connection with population and wealth. Pareto noticed that 80% of Italy's land was owned by 20% of the population. He then carried out surveys on a variety of other countries and found, to his surprise, that a similar distribution applied.

This rule/observation has been applied in various fields such as business where: 80% of your profits come from 20% of your customers.

I believe this rule/observation can also be applied to your studies. However, you should take caution when doing so. Although referred to as a rule, I would be more cautious and refer to it as an observation. This is because it came about as a result of one man's observation. It is not like gravity, which is a natural law that says, "what goes up must come down".

The 80/20 rule can be applied during the revision period. The trick is to make sure you have covered the crucial 20% of any exam, as this is likely to account for 80% of your result. There are various ways of finding the crucial 20%. One of them is to utilise the office hours of academic staff in your department, as we discussed above. Another way is to view past papers and make a list of the types of questions that usually get asked.

Past papers can be an indication of what is likely to come up in the exam. However I would advise a lot of caution on this as examiners may change the format of the exam. That said, examiners may be limited in the questions they can ask, simply because some topics yield more questions than others.

Getting the right perspective

It is important to put everything in its rightful place. Being part of a Campus ministry, Jesus Alive Fellowship, I really believe that "seeking God first and living righteously" can benefit all areas of your life, including your studies. Getting the right perspective involves seeing success the same way God sees it.

I have come to realize that getting a first isn't everything. As I have mentioned before, it's not what you know, but who you know that matters. You could have the highest grades in your class, but may struggle to get an internship/graduate job. I have realized that God is the best person you could ever know, he can give you favour no matter what your grade. This is because he has the power. According to Proverbs 21v1 "The king's heart is like a stream of water directed by the Lord; he guides it wherever he pleases."

I have found out that, even when I have failed to get what I want (academically), there is still a bigger purpose behind it. I have come to the conclusion that you don't necessarily need a first class degree to have a successful career. I know that, even without it, God will open doors for you that a first class can't. However, this doesn't mean that you shouldn't aim for a first class when you graduate.

Having this attitude will be very useful when dealing with disappointment. Knowing that God has greater plans for you can motivate you to maintain a positive attitude towards your degree. You will be able to prevent previous failures from affecting your future successes.

Aptitude

Definition: An inherent or acquired capacity for something.

I believe that far too much emphasis is placed on factors like memory and natural intelligence when it comes to studying. Although these factors are important, there is so much more that goes into getting a good degree.

For example, it doesn't take natural intelligence to meet a crucial deadline; it requires planning and time-management. It also doesn't take natural intelligence to deal with exam stress; it takes a positive mental attitude developed over the academic year to calm exam nerves.

I hope you are beginning to see that aptitude, although important, isn't everything.

That said, there are several ways to improve your aptitude; libraries contain a whole host of books which you could borrow to help increase your natural aptitude:

- Critical Thinking Skills – Stella Cottrell
- The Exam Skills Handbook – Stella Cottrell
- The Study Skills Handbook – Stella Cottrell

As a preview to the next chapter, it is important to note that there is a distinction between natural aptitude and God-given aptitude. The former is a result of our inherited abilities from our parents. This applies to everyone, irrespective of their character or faith. The latter, however, applies to those with the same kind of character and level of faith as Daniel, Shadrach, Meshach and Abednego.

According to Daniel 1v17a, "God gave these four young men an unusual aptitude for understanding every aspect of literature and wisdom". Our efforts in the next chapter will be spent investigating what led God to bestow such a blessing on them, in the hope that we too can appropriate the same blessings.

CHAPTER 7

The Daniel Experiment

In natural sciences, hypotheses are tested by conducting controlled experiments. For example, to investigate whether paracetamol helps with headaches, we randomly allocate a large number of otherwise-similar subjects with headaches into either a treatment or a control group. The treatment group receives the paracetamol, whilst the control group receives the placebo, an apparently identical - but actually inactive - pill.

We then observe whether there is an improvement in the headaches of the treatment group relative to the control group. If the answer is yes, we can conclude, with caution, that the paracetamol has a palliative effect on headaches. This has to be the case, since in this experiment; all other conditions were kept the same between the two groups.

This method of conducting controlled experiments is not a recent idea. It has been carried out throughout the ages. Arguably the earliest record of such experiments is recorded in the book Daniel, which was written in 535 B.C., approximately.

Background

The book is set in Babylon (known today as Iraq), which was ruled by King Nebuchadnezzar. He was a cruel leader, who took delight in torturing his victims and - in an effort to expand his empire - conquered surrounding nations. Among the captives taken from one of these nations were four young men (commonly known as Daniel, Shadrach, Meshach and Abednego), who were deported to Babylon, where they were among the chosen few who were to be trained in the language and literature of Babylon and would later enter royal service.

The story has surprising similarities with student experiences at uni:

- Daniel and his friends were to be trained for three years – similar to the length most degree courses

- For the four young men, Babylon was away from home – similarly, most uni students live away from home whilst completing their degree.

- After the training they would enter the royal service – similarly, after uni, we enter the real world.

As the story goes, Daniel and his friends abstained from eating the food provided by the king, in an effort to avoid being defiled. Daniel and his friends asked the person who was in charge of them if they could have only vegetables and water instead of the luxurious foods that were given to the others.

From Daniel 1v15-17 we find that, "at the end of the ten days they looked healthier and better nourished than any of the young men who ate the royal food. So the guard took away their choice food and the wine they were to drink and gave them vegetables instead. To these four young men God gave knowledge and understanding of all kinds of literature and learning. And Daniel could understand visions and dreams of all kinds."

It was after reading this scripture that I wanted to undergo a similar regime, in order to get the same blessings that Daniel and his friends received. I wanted "an unusual aptitude for understanding every aspect of literature and wisdom". True to His word, God gave me and my friends the same blessings that He gave Daniel and his friends.

Testimonies

Tino, BSc Economics

During my second year at uni, I made several observations about my studies. Prior to the Daniel Fast I was just about averaging a first class. There were times I foolishly thought that God could just do the work for me. As a result, I ended up getting my second lowest mark for an assessed work, at 54%. Apart from proving that you need to put in the work, it also serves to illustrate that you don't need a first in every exam or assignment to end up with a first overall.

During the Easter holiday, just before the third term, I was wondering how I could increase my grades without reducing the amount of time I spent doing God's work. I then came across the Daniel Fast.

Together with Jessica and Christina, I undertook it with the aim of proving that you don't have to reduce the amount of time you spend in God's presence just to get a higher mark. The fast lasted for 10 days and, as a result, my exam experience was so peaceful.

Overall, the exam period wasn't difficult, it was rather relaxing and, what was strange was that when exams had finished, I didn't get that huge feeling of relief that exams had finally finished. This is because I didn't feel like I had even started. Strangely, this was one of the most exciting periods of my second year.

During my second exam, I really felt that God was with me. The previous night I had been revising a topic and was failing to understand it. It just seemed like I wasn't making any progress and proved to be a bit frustrating. During that evening, I felt that I hardly had any time to do other things, let alone pray. However, a friend came over, who needed some prayer. Initially all I was thinking about was my exam, which was the next day. However, my housemates and I prayed for her and after that we shared our encounters with God, which brought a lot of peace to me.

In the morning, hours before my exam, I was frantically revising the same topic, but it just wasn't going in. So in the end I put it into God's hands. I felt within myself that he was going to be with me in the exam. So I went to the exam hall, and for the first time in my life, I was not confident in a topic that was part of the crucial 20% (see above). Namely, it was guaranteed that the question would show up – and show up it did. However, as if out of nowhere, I finally started to understand the topic. Having struggled the previous night and in the few hours before the actual exam, I really felt that God was with me.

As I was answering the question, aspects of the topic that I didn't know suddenly started making sense. It was amazing! Thus, after the fast, my average was a stronger first than prior to the fast. I sincerely believe that God gave me an aptitude for learning and understanding, simply because I chose to put him first. The purpose for this is to say that, when it comes to the exam period, don't forsake God.

Jessica, BA Economics with French
Alongside the hours I had put into my revision time, I believed that this fast would enable me to furthermore improve my end of the year grade. However, I had to understand that I also had to do my part by actually revising, since faith without works is dead (James 2v17)

It was particularly challenging, because I had never done anything like it before and it was very different to my usual dieting habits. I conducted the fast out of faith; I had to believe that it was going to work; otherwise it would have been just a change in eating habits (Hebrews 11v1). Apart from my change in diet, a constant meditation on the word and constant prayer were as important.

Results: In my first year, my approach and effort towards my education were more relaxed, simply because I was aware of the 40% pass mark. Also, there were modules which I did not particularly enjoy; consequently my work-ethic was not the greatest. My overall grade for my 1st year at University was a mid 2.2 at 56%.

In my second year I was more determined and ambitious to work harder and so I invested more time in studying. I generally worked harder throughout the year and my coursework grades were much better. I enjoyed my course more, as I was given the opportunity to choose most of the modules; it is fair to say that my modules in my second year were much harder than in my first year.

During my summer exams I felt so much peace, even when things didn't go according to plan! I sincerely believe that this was due to the fast. Although I had invested a lot of time in my revision in preparation for the summer exams, my performance was not the greatest. My coursework grades were good enough to balance my overall grade and my overall grade for my 2nd year at University was a mid 2.1 at 64% - a substantial growth, which I honestly believe was due the fast.

Christina, BA International development

During the fast I was in debt to the university and knew that I would not be allowed to sit my summer examinations. However, my Heavenly Father had good plans for my life and by His grace my revision didn't go to waste and I was allowed to sit my exams.

During the fast, I sensed the growth of a selfless faith, one where my alarm would go off and I would actually get up instead of pressing the snooze button five times before I woke up an hour later. It was a time where my student job, my modules and I were not the centre of everything. Instead, it was one where I gladly found solace in seeking God's word, where He was the centre of my life and the little meaningless things that mattered before were no longer as important.

I found it interesting how things have worked out in my life since the fast. It was not as though God and I made a deal where I would deprive myself from certain foods and my life would supernaturally improve; I had to turn away from my sinful ways, from the 'little' and 'lazy/harmless' habits that accumulated and eventually brought along greater ones. I had to learn not to compromise with my faith, my responsibilities, my relationships or anything that would jeopardize the God in me. I had to learn how to obey my God and his ways (Jeremiah 7v23).

Surely, after depriving my body of so many foods, I identified numerous changes! Firstly, my face was glowing (yes girls, it was ... and I dare say it still is)! I was happier! I was more confident! I liked Oat Milk!

Academically, I was not worried about my examinations and, with constant prayer, I was able to discipline myself and work with other students. I was able to go to sleep knowing that I had studied enough for the day and that I would not relive the nightmare of 2010 - where I merely passed with a 3rd.

Spiritually, I was, and still am, an entirely different person. My relationship with the Father has grown from strength to strength and climbed from glory to glory! I have allowed Him into my life and He came in, even though I am not worth it! I was speaking authority over my life and believing it.

Looking back, I can proudly say that He brought me through! All my grades improved, I got a 2:1 in my second year and my debt has been settled. I pray that through my testimony, many can relate with where I was and where I currently am, and that we all continue to aspire for the best and dream big, because in Him all things are possible!

Bigger picture

It can be easy to solely focus on the academic blessings God bestowed on the four Hebrew boys and fail to see the bigger picture. In my second year, I was solely focused on the academic blessings and I missed the spiritual and financial blessings God also gave to the four.

In particular, at the end of the ten days, alongside the academic blessings, Daniel 1 v17b says, 'and God gave Daniel the special ability to interpret the meanings of visions and dreams'. As with any type of fast, we should be drawn nearer to God and this allows Him to bless us with spiritual blessings.

Moreover, Daniel and his friends received financial blessings, as God gave them the opportunity to impress their employer, King Nebuchadnezzar (Daniel 1v18-19). For a lot of graduates, finding employment is very difficult given the current competition within the market. However if God can bestow such favour on these four Hebrew boys, He can certainly do it for us.

After doing the 10 day Daniel fast the second time round, with the bigger picture in mind, I witnessed God's providence. On the last day of the fast, within the space of eight hours, I received two calls and an email, all from different companies, with positive replies concerning the various job applications I had made. To me, that was a signal that God had acknowledged the fast.

There are various guidelines surrounding the fast, however the most important thing is the state of your heart during the period. I believe that any form of fasting is a way to humble the heart and guess what? God gives more grace to the humble.

During this period aim to develop your relationship with God, through reading His word and spending more time in His presence through secret prayer. All of this will pay huge dividends when it comes to actually writing the exam. A useful website to learn more about the fast can be found in the endnotes corresponding to this chapter.

PART 3

Maturity

CHAPTER 8

Pursuit of God

For many Christian students, going to uni is an opportunity to meet people of the same faith. This can often make expressing one's faith easier, as the weight of "persecution" can be shared. In other words, to coin a new phrase, "many Christians make light persecution". This can be achieved through sharing common experiences and encouraging each other within Christian societies on campus.

That said, a large proportion of Christians, 47.5% to be exact, would rather keep their Christianity a secret, according to the research by Yap, Keenan and Page (2011). Whilst researching material for the book, I came across an article from the Guardian, with Q&A's about fresher's week. One student asked for the following advice "I don't like getting blind drunk, so I've been hanging out with the non-drinkers. They seem like a nice bunch, but yesterday I went to a barbecue with them and it was held at a church. Turns out they're all really, really Christian. Help."

Clearly the fact that they were Christians was distressing for the student. This should come as no surprise, as according to 2 Corinthians 2v15–16a, "Our lives are a Christ-like fragrance rising up to God. But this fragrance is perceived differently by those who are being saved and by those who are perishing. To those who are perishing, we are a dreadful smell of death and doom."

No matter how much we excel in areas common to both believers and non believers, such as intelligence, wealth and likeability or sobriety and niceness, as identified by the distressed student, the world is always going to be put off by our "dreadful smell of death and doom" and they will cry "help" or, at least, avoid us. I understand that I am making broad conclusions from this single incidence. However the truth is that we are all going to face this at one level or another.

I believe that this is among the main reasons why many Christians may be reluctant to disclose their faith, especially at uni. It is true that everyone wants to be accepted, hence some Christians may conform and hide the "dreadful smell of death and doom" in fear of alienating people and not being accepted. However, in John 15 v 19, Jesus said that, "the world would love you as one of its own if you belonged to it, but you are no longer part of this world. I chose you to come out of the world, so it hates you".

Interestingly, in response to the distressed student's plea for help, 'Uncle Freshers' uses the phrase "Trojan Christians". For those that don't know the story of the Trojan horse here is a brief explanation. This comes at no extra fee, apart from paying close attention to the bigger picture.

After a fruitless 10-year siege between the Greeks and the city of Troy, the Greeks constructed a huge wooden horse and hid a select force of 30 men inside. The Greeks pretended to sail away and the Trojans pulled the horse into their city as a victory trophy. That night, the Greek force crept out of the horse and opened the gates for the rest of the Greek army, which had sailed back under cover of night. The Greek army entered and destroyed the city of Troy, decisively ending the war.

The bigger picture is one of deception and crafty intention, similar to an image of a wolf dressed in sheep's clothing. By coining the phrase "Trojan Christians", we can quickly conclude that "Uncle Freshers" is portraying Christians in a similar light. He then goes on to advise the distressed student to "be strong, for this is but a test".

At most, "Uncle Freshers" is saying, "don't let them impose their beliefs on you and force you to convert to their faith". At the very least he is saying, "don't let their lifestyles convert you to their faith". The truth probably lies somewhere in the middle. However what is certain is that individuals who are *"really, really Christian"* will often be viewed as deceptive or crafty. In 1 Peter 2v12, we are told, "Be careful to live properly among your unbelieving neighbours. Then even if they accuse you of doing wrong, they will see your honourable behaviour, and they will give honour to God when he judges the world".

Enemy tries to silence you

For a lot of us, as Christians, we often experience seasons during which we either feel empowered and strong in the Lord or simply defeated and helpless. This manifests itself in varying degrees for different individuals. However, in seasons where a Christian feels defeated and helpless, for whatever reason, the result is that their level of impact on the campus is significantly reduced.

The enemy will stop at nothing to hinder your pursuit of God, regardless of your calling or level of faith. In fear of the good things that will come out of the Pursuit of God, the enemy will try to silence you.

Every so often you hear the excuse, 'I don't feel worthy enough to go to church or a gathering of believers'. Here, the enemy uses guilt to prevent us from pursuing God. Pursuing God doesn't mean that we never make mistakes. If that were so, why would we need to pursue Him at all? Rather, pursuing God means we are constantly focused on Him, instead of focusing on ourselves and our mistakes.

Pursuing God at uni involves being a light to your campus. More often than not, the enemy tries to silence us from preaching the gospel, by making us feel unworthy. The devil is called the accuser (Revelations 12 v10). Very often he discourages us from preaching the good news by accusing us of being "hypocrites".

The first few verses in Jeremiah 1 illustrate God's heart for the advancement of His word. As the story goes, God had given several messages to Jeremiah the Prophet, which He wanted nations and kingdoms to hear. In response, the youthful Jeremiah responded, 'I can't speak for you! I'm too young!'. However God replied. "Don't say, 'I'm too young', for you must go wherever I send you and say whatever I tell you". Often, we feel like we are "too this" or "too that" or that "we did this" or "we did that", so much so that we are too focused on what we are and what we have done. As a result, we feel unable to share God's word. Yet all the while, God says, "Don't say, 'I'm too [fill in the rest]".

The good news is not about what we have done; rather it is about Jesus Christ. It's about what He has done and is doing in us. You are not preaching about how good you are; rather, you can use what God is doing in your life as a point of evangelism.

John Piper, one of the most prominent preachers of our time, has preached on the importance of preaching the gospel to yourself. As Christians, we need to remind ourselves of the sacrifice that Jesus made for us through His death, burial and resurrection. This will empower us in our Pursuit of God, as we proclaim the gospel to our campus and the outside world.

The enemy will also try to slow down your Pursuit of God through spiritual attacks. These are often aimed at preventing you from operating in your spiritual gifts. In Ephesians 6v12, the Bible says, 'For we are not fighting against flesh and blood enemies but against evil rulers and authorities of the unseen world, against mighty powers in this dark world, and against evil spirits in the heavenly places". Furthermore, in 2 Corinthians 10v4 (NIV), we are told that, "The weapons we fight with are not the weapons of the world. On the contrary, they have divine power to demolish strongholds." The gift of prophecy is one such weapon. The enemy has been known to come in the form of dreams, in an attempt to intimidate believers away from using their gifts to the benefit of others. In other cases, the sense of a dark presence has also been reported.

In whatever way the enemy tries to silence you, "In all these things we are more than conquerors through Him who loved us" (Romans 8v37). Pursuing God at uni is not an easy task. However at the end of our time at uni, we will look back over it with great joy, knowing that it wasn't in vain.

Observation

Hypothesis: Some Christian students hide their faith; In a study conducted by Andrew Kam-Tuck Yip, Michael Keenan and Sarah-Jane Pag, called " Religion, Youth and Sexuality: Selected Key Findings from a Multi-faith Exploration" They found that 47.3% of the 213 Christian students in the survey hide their faith.

Unexpected text message

A few weeks have gone by and the six students are getting to know each other quite well. The students regularly have topical debates and get to understand where they each stand on certain issues.

Over issues like abortion and assisted suicide, Chris always refers to his core philosophy "live and let live". The other students are also quick to vocalise their views on these issues. However Emmanuel hasn't made any effort to voice his views on anything, so far. Coming from a Christian background, he hasn't spoken about his faith at all.

Early the next morning, he received an encouraging word, in the form of a text. Immediately, two things stood out. Firstly, it was not from one of his contacts; "maybe it's an old friend, whose number I haven't got any more", he says to himself. Secondly, and more intriguing, is the way the text message ends, with, "If you aren't ashamed to do this, please pass this on. Jesus said, 'If you are ashamed of me, I will be ashamed of you before my Father".

Upon reading this, Emmanuel's heart starts racing at a similar pace to when he had the moral dilemma of getting drunk or not. Without knowing that the walls have ears, Emmanuel says to himself; "I know a few people that need to read this, but they might think I am being overly religious."

What would Joseph do?

He would stick to his guns, even if it meant standing alone. In the introduction to this chapter we understood that people often hide their faith for fear of being rejected. I can empathise with this, as I too wanted to be accepted. However I believe that, your true friends will accept you for how you are. If this isn't the case, then it's not worth compromising yourself in order to be accepted.

Instead, find people that will accept you, and will respect that which you value in life. You are more likely to find such friends within Christian societies, assuming that your faith is what you value most in life. However, be aware that not every Christian has your best interests at heart. You may even have non-believing friends who may care more about your values than some Christians. Sad, but true.

Disclaimer: So often on online social networks, you come across Biblical messages or images which say, 'If you love God, share this message'. Not sharing the message doesn't mean that you don't love God. Acting out of obligation is not a sign of true love; this is because free will is not fully exercised.

Experiment

- Participate in group evangelism, over time you will find it easier to share your faith.

- Preach the gospel to yourself as often as you can

- Whilst studying, challenge yourself to have your bible out among your text books, this could initiate a conversation where you can share your faith.

CHAPTER 9

Prayer and Evangelism

From the previous Bible studies I've had whilst at university, regarding prayer, it is often described as a two way communication between man and God. Our earthly relationships teach us that communication creates intimacy. I believe that you became attached to whatever you make yourself vulnerable to. Making yourself vulnerable to someone can be done through sharing your deepest secrets; as a result, the other person begins seeing you for who you are. This paves the way for bonds to be created; we can call this emotional intimacy.

It is not surprising therefore that, if we don't spend much time communicating with God, we won't develop any intimacy with Him. God desires to be intimate with us; He desires to communicate with us on a frequent basis (1 Thessalonians 5v17).

There have been times when I have craved to feel the presence of God, but haven't spent enough time in His presence. In Matthew 26 v 40-41, whilst praying in the garden of Gethsemane, Jesus "returned to the disciples and found them asleep. He said to Peter, Couldn't you watch with me *even one hour*? Keep watch and pray, so that you will not be given in to temptation. For the spirit is willing, but the body is weak!"

It comes as no surprise to see statistics like "the average time Christians spend praying is between 3 and 7 minutes a day, including prayer at meal times." Although we may cast doubts on the accuracy of this, there is no getting away from the fact that prayer is by and large neglected. Having been part of the Prayer and Evangelism department within a Christian society at uni, I have observed this. Even as part of the prayer team, there were times when I relied solely on the society's prayer meetings to really "watch and pray" as Jesus commanded, instead of doing so by myself.

In writing this chapter, I felt God telling me that I shouldn't expect His manifestation, if I am not willing to spend time in His presence. It's not that we are incapable of experiencing His presence; rather, we just haven't done the necessary things to be able to experience His presence.

According to Gay-Lynn Taylor in an article, "Too busy for God?", the author argues that "our busyness can distract us from God". As students, it is all too easy to "become absorbed in the world's agendas and society's temptations, and without even realising it, we can neglect to spend precious time with God in our lives." Although the article is targeted at Law Students, it's applicable to students of all disciplines, assuming they desire to be close to God. According to the author, busyness is an excuse that many students give for not spending quiet time with God. "As students, coursework deadlines, exam revision, job and work experience applications [...] social lives and sports commitments, all mean that time is precious."

As a result, students "attempt to squeeze in ten minutes of somewhat half-hearted prayer or Bible study on a busy tube or even a token ten minutes before bed with our prayers more commonly becoming our dreams." The author then concludes that "Unfortunately the reality is that we do this, more often than not, to appease our guilty consciences rather than as the out working of a genuine desire to deepen our relationship with God."

I believe that Christianity is about relationship with God, rather than a mere religion. If prayer starts becoming more of a chore than a pleasure, then it is no longer about relationship. That said, there will be times were Christianity may seem like a religion (refer to James 1v26). With regards to prayer, sometimes to have relationship with God, you have to be "religious", but which I mean if you label forcing yourself to wake up early in order to pray as religious. It is to my mind a risk worth taking, to be labelled as "religious" in order to discipline ourselves to "watch and pray".

Testimonies

Unusual Prayer Meeting

Sarah, BSc Psychology

The Spirit, through our leader, directed our society to watch and pray. Up until then, I hadn't realised the importance of having a sense of urgency for God. However, after the unusual prayer meeting that we had, I really understand it now.

We had a week of prayer, where we would meet in the morning to pray whilst under a fast. Throughout the week, the Spirit directed us all in different ways and as a result of those five days, and in particular the last day, my spiritual life will never be the same. I can't explain the growth of my spiritual woman in words. All I can say is thank God I didn't miss out. We all started off not being truly expectant, but I believe all our hearts have changed and we have all received a new and fresh anointing.

Tino, BSc Economics

For me, the unusual prayer meeting, started with a sermon titled 'Pray and be alone with God', by Paul Washer. I had listened to it a month previous to the prayer meeting. God was calling me to more prayer and fasting. He confirmed this through one of the pastors at my home church, who gave a message titled 'Sixty minutes of prayer'. I am grateful to God that I obeyed. I am also grateful to God that, other individuals who He had previously also called to pray and fast, also obeyed.

Before the unusual prayer meeting, we had all been praying and fasting as a society. We would meet up early in the morning and pray together and then get on with our day. Friday, the last day of the fast, seemed like just another day; nothing could have prepared us for the kind of encounter we had with God.

For a lot of people, waking up that morning seemed unusually difficult. It's as if the enemy knew what would take place in the meeting. I can probably count on two hands how many prayer meetings I've had, since becoming born again, where God moved so strongly.

What was meant to be an hour long prayer meeting, quickly turned into about a two hour long desperation cry out to God. What was meant to be a prayer meeting with a structure of what would happen and when, soon become a spontaneous occasion where everyone present was vulnerable to the promptings of the Spirit. Never had I seen such zeal and desperation for God amongst young people, it was a beautiful sight.

These are the kind of prayer meetings that help bring revival on campus, as after the meeting, everyone felt empowered by the Spirit. Some even felt bold enough to shout out the name of Jesus while walking to the campus library; something rather unthinkable in the absence of such empowerment.

Evangelism

I have heard it said that "evangelism is the only thing we can do on earth that we can't do in heaven". I totally agree with this statement and it is important for us as Christians to be a light on our campus. In Matthew 28 v 20, Jesus gave the great commission to His disciples in saying, "go and make disciples of all nations, baptising them in the name of the Father and the Son and the Holy Spirit."

The great thing about uni, as someone pointed out in view of the great commission, is that all nations come to you. Today's universities are largely cosmopolitan; rich with different cultures and languages. This gives us Christians the opportunity to witness to such individuals, who may end up taking the gospel back to their country.

I have put prayer and evangelism together, because I believe that you can't have one without the other. Prayer empowers us to evangelise, through conviction or boldness. Evangelism gives us a cause to pray for lost souls or against spiritual strongholds (2 Corinthians 10v4)

My Pastor in Colchester, who I have to say has been a real blessing to me, has always encouraged us to "Get the Father's heart". I believe that prayer empowers us to evangelise because it enables us to "Get the Father's heart". It is through communicating with Father God that we develop a burden for the lost. In Ezekiel 18v23 we read, "Do you think that I like to see wicked people die? Says the Sovereign Lord. Of course not! I want them to turn from their wicked ways and live". When we spend enough time in God's presence we develop a conviction and the kind of boldness that will help us when we evangelise, either to our flatmates, people around campus, or people on the same course as us.

Personal Evangelism - Faith, works

This is an excerpt from the article entitled "Faith, Works", which I wrote for Chosen Generation Ministries in August 2011. To find the full article please go to cgministries.co.uk. In writing the article, I included a testimony of my experience whilst evangelising at uni. It reads as follows:

On many occasions, during evangelism, I have come to realise that faith without works really is dead. This hasn't always been the case. Before I came to understand this, I would always find a barrier during evangelism. What was particularly frustrating about this barrier was that it was the same on every occasion. It would always leave me speechless and unable to progress.

When evangelising, I would always begin by introducing myself and getting to know the other person. I would then ask questions to get the person to think about spiritual things. Such questions included, "Have you been to church before?" or "Do you believe you are a good person?" These questions would conveniently lead to other questions.

However whenever I asked the question, "Do you believe in God?" it did either one of two things. If the person said "no", I would then go on to talk about why they should believe in God (the easy part). However if the person said, "yes, I do believe in God", I often had nothing else to say apart from "Thank you and God bless you". This was particularly frustrating, especially because, for a lot of people, they just said "yes", so that I could leave them quicker (lol).

However I have now come to realise that, "even the demons believe" (James 2v19c). Merely believing isn't enough, as some seem to think.

As a result of this realisation, I have started to ask people who say they believe in God the following question: "How does believing in God affect your daily choices?" This is an important question that we all need to think about. We can't get away with just believing.

"Faith by itself isn't enough. Unless it produces good deeds (James 2v17)"

CHAPTER 10
Maturity

A University Chaplain's perspective

I've been asked to give you my perspective as a University Anglican Chaplain on maturity and spirituality for young students. If you are aged between 18 and 21 and you are at university for the first time, this is probably the last thing on your mind! However, the fact that you have read so far is a great sign that you are someone who is interested and curious about yourself, and would like to discover more of what makes you tick as a person.

I will begin with what seems like an obsolete question: Why did you come to University? For some of us, coming to university has been a culmination of hard work, determination and the desire to succeed in our chosen area of study. For others, coming to university is just a way of escaping the parents, home and siblings who bother us. Still more for some, coming to university may not have been a choice – it may have been a decision made for us by our parents, or we ourselves couldn't decide what to do with the next stage of life, so we ended up at University. We may feel excited, elated, sad, happy, confused, frightened or angry or have mixed emotions all at the same time.

The reason why I have raised the question of why you have come to university is because thinking about our reasons for being at university may help us to think about what is important to us, and perhaps what we need to do next in order to get the best experience out of university life and one day, beyond university. Part of maturity means examining our lives so that we do not walk in the dark.

University will be a time when our assumptions, prejudices (yes, we all have them!), lifestyles and worldview gets challenged. Unless you have chosen to live as a hermit in your student dig, you will inevitably meet people from all over the world – with different cultures, faiths, thought processes, and ways of relating. So, we may find that what we thought was "normal" turns out to be extremely unusual for other people. These challenges will prompt us to question ourselves – why do I think/feel/act the way I do? Why do I feel so strongly about one issue but not about another? What is the meaning of my life? These are all important questions.

In such a bewildering environment, we may come to rely on our new-found university friends to help us think about our questions. However, after some time, we may come to realise our friends are just in the same predicament as we are – trying to figure out what life means, how life works, and where they are heading! This is why it is important at this early stage of our university life that we think about spiritual and maturational support from outside of our immediate circle – to help us identify and achieve our goals of being a mature and dynamic individual.

One of the great ways we can do this is through mentors, counsellors/psychotherapists, university Chaplains or spiritual advisors. Let me clarify what they are and how they may be of help to you.

Chaplains

Chaplains are usually ordained ministers (this means they have under-gone theological and pastoral training and have been approved by their church denomination e.g. Anglican, Baptist, Free Church etc.) They are usually based at the University Chaplaincy/Faith/Spiritual/Student support centre. Their job is to look after student's spiritual well-being (this means they should be praying for you, making sure you have good biblical advice, be listening to you, and in times of need, be arranging ways to help you e.g. from drinking a cup of tea with you to arranging support for you over-night if you were critically ill and alone). Depending on the Chaplain, they may have other training and qualifications such as spiritual mentoring alongside being a pastoral person.

Mentors

Mentors are usually people who are experienced in navigating some of the challenges of life. They can be someone we look up to, and someone who is good at helping us to develop our personalities. A good mentor is someone who can help us to discover what we are passionate about, keep us motivated about what we want to achieve, help us to see different ways of doing things, give us advice about our ways of working and most importantly, not be afraid to gently push us forward when we are reluctant to move forward! Typically, a mentoring session takes place informally once a month or more (depending on personal agreement), usually with a cuppa and may have social elements to it (such as going to an event together). You can ask someone informally to be your mentor – such as a mature Christian in church whom you want to learn from! However, mentoring can also be a professional arena and there are Christian mentors who are specially trained to provide mentoring as a professional service.

For example, some Christian colleges provide training in mentoring: *http://www.cliffcollege.ac.uk/page/certificate_in_christian_mentoring_and_coaching*

Counsellors/Psychotherapists

Counsellors or Psychotherapists are professionals who are trained and qualified in helping us to explore why we feel and behave in the way we do. They are trained to help give you space to process difficult feelings you may have, or to help you make sense of things that are confusing or unmanageable for you. They are great for helping you to reflect about your own life and how you can make a change. Unlike mentoring, therapy is a specific relationship that does NOT include advice-giving, or socialising, or having a cup of tea and chatter. Rather, the relationship is a non-judgemental, confidential and highly thoughtful time together, usually for 50 minutes once-a-week for at least 8 sessions or more. Counsellors and Therapists should help you to think through for yourself what you want to do, and to help you find new ways of thinking and being. A good counsellor or therapist will not be afraid to challenge you when necessary, but will always do so within a trusting relationship. They are usually accredited/registered by professional bodies. For example,

- BACP (British Association of Counselling and Psychotherapy) *http://www.itsgoodtotalk.org.uk/*
- ACC (Association of Christian Counsellors)
- *http://www.acc-uk.org/*

These professional bodies register the counsellors and therapists so that they adhere to professional ethical standards. This means that if you were unhappy with what was provided, you can make a formal complaint to these bodies.

Proactive Thought and Action

Many people think you have to be seriously in need before you can contact the Chaplain, Mentor or Counsellor/Psychotherapist but in fact, it is really helpful to have such support right at the start of your university life. That way, you are already one step ahead in terms of preparing for your future and for your walk with God.

It is perhaps worthwhile at this point reflecting on what stops us from asking for what we need. Here are some of them:

- *Shame* - Nobody experiences what I experience – it is too embarrassing – much better to try to forget it.
- *Guilt* - I am the one who did it, I am the one who made the situation worse, so I can't ask for it.
- *Fear* - What will he/she think of me? It's just too much!
- *Pride* - I can cope perfectly OK on my own. I should be able to do everything without asking for help.
- *Despair* - No one can really help me, It's just pointless. I can't go on.

Case examples

(Please note that all names and details have been changed in order to preserve confidentiality)

Richard Brown

Richard is a 19 year old second year student who came to see me as a Chaplain at the university. At one level, he was really happy and busy – studying, socialising and doing lots of sports. However, at another level, Richard was bothered about some things in his life - the conversation led to Richard disclosing that he sometimes feels that he was too busy and this meant that he did not have much time for closer relationships and occasionally, Richard feels quite lonely even when he is in the middle of a crowd. Richard is a Christian, but he also found it difficult to develop his spiritual life. He found that his prayer times often felt uninspiring for him and he would give up on them.

The conversation revealed much about Richard's life, and as a result, we were able to look together at what would be the most helpful way for him to grow in his relationships with other people and with God. We decided that we would meet once a month to talk about his progress. At each session, I would suggest different ways of finding time for himself, and to ensure that he pays attention to what was going on inside of him. What was his "busyness" about? How did his lifestyle affect his relationships? We also explored what was important for Richard when it comes to praying – and I suggested different ways of praying. As the sessions progressed, Richard became better at keeping the balance in his life and making sure that he develops his inner life – and subsequently, he also started dating! Richard also found that the best way for him to pray was not inside a building on a chair, but outdoors whilst jogging! As a result of these discoveries, Richard has become more mature and whole as a person – he was able to fulfil his full potential.

Sarah Grey

Sarah was a 20 year old third-year student. She first approached the counsellor because Sarah has been feeling depressed for the last three months. As she talked with her counsellor, it soon emerged that Sarah was also addicted to sex with men and to drinking. This would often take over her life to the extent that she could not study or concentrate on anything important. Sarah is a Christian, but feels that God is very far away from her, and she feels she has lost her faith as a result. The therapist listened very carefully to Sarah, especially about her painful experiences of sleeping with men and then waking up with regrets, and her drinking episodes. Over her regular sessions, the therapist explored the meaning beneath her addictions. For Sarah, this means discovering that her deep need to have a sense of Self and to be connected to people has become sexualised – and she was able to gradually change her way of relating to men with the help of her therapist. Sarah also began to attend an AA (Alcoholic Anonymous) group in which she was able to process her addiction to drinking – she realised that her drinking was a form of "covering up" of her pain. In addition, Sarah consulted the Chaplain about being in a prayer group to help her reconnect with her faith in God. Over the year, Sarah's life began to change, and she became happier and more contented with her life. She recently commented that it felt like her life has changed like a "black-and-white" TV to a full colour TV.

Where is God in all of this?

University is a great place for discovering the truth that God is really who He says He is in Christ. He is really faithful (We discover that he really stays with us through thick and thin), Strong (able to help us when we most need it), Loving (so I don't need to chase after it from men or women around me to feel loved). It is an adventure if you have God right from the start of your university life! In response, you may begin to discover what it means to Love the LORD your God with all your heart, your mind, your will and your soul. One way of looking at this is like a check-list:

Hallmarks of health

Physically (Mind)

- Am I eating 5 a day? Or missing food? Or is it all fast food?
- Am I exercising regularly
- Am I having good sleeping habits?
- What is my alcohol level intake?

Emotionally (Heart)

- Being in community – includes sports, social groups
- Learning accountability – talking and praying
- Being part of the Church – worshipping etc.
- Mentor?
- Counsellor/Psychotherapist?

Spiritually (Soul)

- Regular set time for prayer
- Being in small group for bible study
- Have a spiritual advisor

If you would like to contact me for more information, or to take up therapy, please contact me on: *revthomas@hotmail.co.uk*

PART 4

Relationships

CHAPTER 11

Just friends at uni

As we saw in chapter three, friendships formed at university are more likely to be stronger than those formed outside. In view of this, we can also make the same conclusion about friendships between people of the opposite sex. However such reasoning begs the following question, "is it possible to be just friends with the opposite sex?"

In my view, I believe that it is possible to be just friends with opposite sex. In my first year, I had five housemates, four of whom were female. We were all quite close and had so much fun. In fact, I write this part of the book two days after catching up with them for dinner at La Tasca. So, even after two years, we still keep in touch and enjoy each other's company. At no point did the "just friends" status ever develop into anything more, as far as I am concerned.

However, such friendships are not immune from developing into "Friends who like each other", as we shall discover later on.

Being just friends with the opposite sex is an opportunity to pursue the gift of singleness. According to Paul in 1 Corinthians 7 v 32b, the gift of singleness allows a person to "spend his time doing the Lord's work and thinking how to please him." I would add that it allows you to be the best that you can be for your future partner. As you will discover, the best way to tell the opposite sex that you care about them, is by being fulfilled in God.

By being fulfilled in God, He develops the traits in you that will make the future relationship successful. For example, He develops in you the patience that will later help you and your partner bear with each other's faults.

Being Fulfilled In God

In Economics we learn how humans respond to scarcity. Namely, "human wants are virtually unlimited. Yet the means of fulfilling human wants are limited." The common conclusion in economics is that people are self-seeking.

As Christians, we may occasionally find ourselves being self-seekers. That is, seeking to please ourselves; seeking satisfaction in things apart from God. We may be seeking satisfaction in a relationship. We may hope for that special someone to come and free us from the apparent "curse" of singleness. However, such a pursuit can often lead to frustration, as nothing will ever satisfy a human heart quite like the Love of God.

Given that humans have "virtually unlimited" wants, your wants can never be satisfied by seeking satisfaction in the opposite sex. This is especially true if the other person is in exactly the same position as you. If you have two people attempting to satisfy each other's unlimited wants, at the very least they will both end up frustrated. At most, they may end up hurting each other.

As Christians, we need to get to a point where we have so much of God's Love within us that we don't need to seek satisfaction in other people. Paul, in his letter to the church at Ephesus, gives us an indication of how we could reach this stage.

He prays a prayer, which contains the keys to being fulfilled in God. This prayer is found in Ephesians 3v16-20:

"I pray that from his glorious, unlimited resources he will empower you with inner strength through his Spirit. Then Christ will make his home in your hearts as you trust in him. Your roots will grow down into God's love and keep you strong. And may you have the power to understand, as all God's people should, how wide, how long, how high, and how deep his love is. May you experience the love of Christ, though it is too great to understand fully. Then you will be made complete with all the fullness of life and power that comes from God. Now all glory to God, who is able, through his mighty power at work within us, to accomplish infinitely more than we might ask or think."

Conveniently, for the purposes of this chapter, Paul uses the phrase "unlimited resources" in reference to God's capacity. Given that the human heart has unlimited wants, only God can satisfy it because only He has unlimited resources. However, we occasionally seek satisfaction in other things, because they give us an instant satisfaction. Unfortunately for us, it is for this very reason that we are never fully satisfied. Instead, when He is working in us through His Spirit, God takes his time.

It takes time because it is long lasting. If it were instant, "your roots wouldn't have enough time to grow down into God's love". The problem is not that God is being slow. Instead, it is simply a natural result, as growth takes a while. However, once your roots have gone deep down, you will be strong: "you will be made complete with all the fullness of life and power that comes from God". You will lack nothing and need not seek satisfaction in anything else apart from in God.

The perfect partner in an imperfect world

Being just friends can easily turn into friends who like each other and this process is safest when the individuals involved are both fulfilled in God. When this is the case, God is more likely to be the focus of the relationship. Thus, when the temptations come, which Paul describes as being "no different from what others experience" (1 Corinthians 10v13), the Grace of God will help "to stand against such evil desires" (James 4v6a).

I strongly believe that great relationships come from great friendships. In choosing a partner, it is common to have a set of criteria which they have to fulfil. Some of the criteria Christian guys have are that she has to sing well, cook well and, of course, she has to be attractive. From conversations I have had with female friends, common preferences include that he must be mature or must speak a certain language and, of course, he must love Jesus.

Although the list could be endless, I have deliberately chosen the above characteristics to illustrate a point. Individuals usually have set criteria in order to find someone who they think they can relate to the most. They may seek in someone characteristics that are similar to their own. For example, English may be a second language, thus they may seek someone who speaks their native language. Suppose that the individual does find such a person? It is easy to see that, although the couple may speak the same native language, they may fail to understand each other.

In Proverbs 27 v 10 (NIV), we are told that "Better a neighbour nearby than a brother far away". Unlike a brother, a neighbour may bear no similarities to us. They may be far from our ideal partner. They may be very different from us; they may have had a very different upbringing to us for example. Sadly, having a set of criteria will exclude such people, even though they may be better suited for you than those who tick all your boxes.

Observation

Hypothesis: Great relationships come from great friendships – This hypothesis is based on the general view that your partner is meant to be your best friend.

Girl talk

It's the end of what has been a very busy week. The girls decide to have a girl's night in and have agreed to order pizza and watch a movie. After deciding on which pizza to order and whose room to use, the girls are yet to decide which movie to watch.

Kemi, in her usual excitement, brings out her large collection of films, "I've got some comedy, romance, rom-com or action". She asks Angela and Janet, "what do you guys wanna watch?" and before they can even answer, she says, "Oooh, how about this film? Love and Basketball! Guys, I think we should watch it!"

Taken aback by Kemi's enthusiasm, the two girls agree to watch the movie. All they need now is the pizza. As they sit in Kemi's room waiting, Angela loses her patience. Out of frustration, she asks, "What's taking them so long? It's almost been 30mins; you would think that they would have delivered it by now."

In response to Angela's frustration and in an effort to kill some time, Kemi suggests having some "girl talk". She asks the two girls, "We might as well have a bonding session. What do you girls look for in a guy?"

Angela is quick to say, "He must be a Christian!", adding, "Confidence also does a lot, there is nothing worse than a man who doesn't know his own mind."

Janet tells the girls that she has already got a man. She tells them how initially he didn't even tick at least half her boxes, but that criteria became less important as she got to know her friend, who is now her boyfriend.

Intrigued by Angela and Janet's answers, Kemi asks that what they think about the guy upstairs. "Who is that?" they reply. "You know. The hot guy upstairs, number 7 on the basketball team." Clueless as to who Kemi is referring to, the two girls tell her that they don't know the guy.

Disappointed at their response and eager to hurry the conversation to another topic, Kemi asks Angela, "How's your man?" Startled at Kemi's directness, Angela answers, "Clearly you know something I don't. Since when did I have a man?"

"Oh come off it", says Janet, as she joins in, adding, "You mean to tell me that a pretty girl like you, hasn't caught the eye of a promising bachelor?"

"Janet, you too?", says Angela, "There is no man or promising bachelor, well at least I don't think there is."

"So there is someone?" asks Kemi.

"Well I am still undecided whether I like him back or not. I mean he is a nice guy and that, cute too, but I don't think I can do it."

"Why not?" asks Kemi

"I really didn't see it coming. I thought he knew the deal. I just wanted to be just friends with him."

"Who is he? Do we know him?" asks Kemi

"Wow, you have so many question to ask don't you?" Angela hesitates and she finally manages to tell Kemi and Angela that it's Emmanuel.

In response to everything that Angela has to say, Janet offers the following advice to her: "A true honest relationship seems to start much slower and can even surprise you. All of a sudden there's this guy who you thought was just a friend, but you can't seem to think about doing anything without him. Those are the keepers."

(To be continued)

What would Joseph do?

One of the greatest love stories, in my opinion, is told in Genesis 29. However, it begins in Genesis 28v1-2, where Isaac the Patriarch instructs his son Jacob, "You must not marry any of these Canaanite women. Instead, go at once to Paddan-aram, to the house of your grandfather Bethuel, and marry one of your uncle Laban's daughters." Upon arriving at Paddan-aram, Jacob met Rachael – Laban's daughter – and immediately embraced her as if to suggest it was love at first sight.

What we should take from this is that, through Isaac, God had instructed Jacob where he would find his wife. Moreover, God also instructed Jacob not to marry any of the Canaanite women, as they could lead him into idol worship. Moreover, within the story, we find a timeless principle; the man should always pursue the woman, and not the other way round. In response, Jacob obeyed without any objection.

Experiment

Making yourself vulnerable before God, since you become attached to what you make yourself vulnerable to. Occasionally, when fasting, make it a must to isolate yourself. This leaves you desperate for human contact, intimacy, comfort, food, and warmth. Instead of getting these from participating in everyday life, by seeking God to fulfil your primary needs, you effectively make yourself vulnerable to Him.

Being fulfilled in God also involves putting a lot of effort into His work. Do things professionally, as you would for things you hold dear, e.g. your studies. Go the extra mile for Him.

Be open and willing to listen to what God has to say about a potential partner. Being just friends with the opposite sex prevents the use of criteria which can exclude potential partners. As a result, you find yourself in contact with more people, without a roving eye. Eventually, you will find the right partner for you and you may be surprised where you find them.

CHAPTER 12

Friends who like each other at uni

Going to university with a view to get into a relationship can prevent you from experiencing all that uni has to offer. It may be that you catch the eye of an on-looking admirer, or perhaps you may be the admirer. Instead of exploring the campus or spending time meeting new people, you may focus your energies on impressing the "hot" guy or girl on the floor above.

Such pursuits seldom have any substance. After a while, when identities have cemented, you may even think to yourself, "What was I thinking, spending all that energy on him or her, when I could have been doing other things."

The best approach is to be open-minded and be yourself. As we saw in the chapter on friendships, "Friendship formed at uni are more likely to be stronger than those formed outside uni". In view of this, revealing your feelings will be a lot easier, at least in theory, so try not to get hung up over this.

Notice I didn't say, "Revealing your feelings will be easy". There is an element of risk that comes with disclosing how you feel about someone.

There is the risk that the other person may not feel the same way. Consequently, this may make things awkward in the friendship. It may or may not take a while for the awkward moment to pass by. However it will, if the friendship is important to both individuals. I strongly believe that the person disclosing the feelings or taking the risk of "rejection" should be the young man and not the young woman, as we learnt in the previous chapter.

In Proverbs 30 v 18 – 19, the writer says, "There are three things that amaze me – no, four things that I don't understand." After listing the first three, he then adds, "How a man loves a woman." The young man is meant to take the initiative; especially since he will one day be the head of the family. Taking this further, think of how unnatural it would be for a woman to propose to a man?

You may be fortunate enough that the feelings are mutual. If you fall into this category, then you are one of the lucky few. There is an added level for Christians, in disclosing your interest in someone of the opposite sex: by revealing your feelings, you are implying that you see yourself spending the rest of your life with that person.

By now we should all have the mind that, when entering into a relationship, we should do so with a view to enter into a life-long covenant in the foreseeable future. Given this added implication, some may take their time in entering into a relationship. More often than not, it's usually the young lady as she wants to be sure that she is with prince charming. So young men, be patient. But ladies, don't let them suffer more than they have to.

Whatever the case, at this stage, both individuals should be mindful of the change in the dynamics of the friendship. At this stage, it is common to start spending more time with the other person. This is where you begin opening up to each other a lot more. At this stage, it becomes evident that starting off as "just friends" is best, as friends accept each other for who they are - warts and all.

It is not unusual, at this stage, for the individuals to give each other constructive criticism in order to build each other up. This process is made so much easier if the individuals are good friends to start off with. Whilst accepting each other, you also want to see the other person be the best they can be. I believe that young ladies are very effective at this and thus play an important role in this matter.

Be mindful

As the friendship progresses, it is certain that challenges will come along. Having too much of a good thing can be a bad thing. As you get closer to someone, you may speak with them so often that there comes a point where a short period without communication may seem unbearable or strange, at the very least. This is evidence that a soul tie is forming.

More than that, you may find yourself more concerned about what you can get out of the friendship instead of what you can give to it. This is evidenced by flattering the other person instead of encouraging them. The former draws their attention towards you, the latter draws their attention towards God.

At this point either individual may start becoming more dependent on the other person than on God. If this is the case, it is usually a sign that a break from the intimate aspect of the friendship is needed. This can be achieved through reducing the amount of time spent together and the number of things you share with each other. This allows you to have clearer judgement.

It doesn't take physical intimacy to create a soul tie, as we read in 1 Samuel 18v1 (NKJV) "the soul of Jonathan was knit to the soul of David, and Jonathan loved him as his own soul". Emotional intimacy will suffice. Namely, spending time with the other person and revealing things about yourself, as the case for David and Jonathan, is enough to create a strong bond between two people.

It been said that if you take a frog and put it in pot with boiling water it will jump out immediately. However, if you take the same frog and put it in a pot filled with cold water and turn on the stove, the frog will remain oblivious to the rising temperature until it's too late and it dies.

Regardless of whether this is true or not, it serves as a good illustration that nothing ever happens overnight. A soul tie is formed over a gradual period of time. It is very important early on to set boundaries and to seek advice, as this will help make your relationship fruitful.

Have a plan

Have a plan for the relationship. What do you want the relationship to accomplish? Are there things that can only be achieved through the relationship? How do you intend on making your relationship a blessing to others? These are important questions, as they give the relationship a greater purpose that goes beyond mere feelings. Furthermore, answers to these questions will act as an encouragement through arguments, temptations, and hurt, to name a few.

A plan is a necessity before becoming accountable to someone. Ideally, whoever you become accountable to will ask you of your intentions in pursing the relationship. This is important for them, because it gives them a rough idea of where the relationship is headed. As a result, they will be better informed to give you the necessary direction.

Moreover, having a plan allows the person to whom you are accountable to regularly check up on you, to find out whether you are keeping to the plan. For example, in your plan you may have set the goal to "avoid kissing". Being accountable to someone will give you an extra incentive to commit to the goal.

Observation

Hypothesis: Emotional intimacy precedes physical intimacy. It is natural to want to share each other's lives. Be it through sharing embarrassing moments, childhood memories and untold secrets. However this can awaken love before the right time, if left unguarded and outside the attention of an accountability figure.

Are you ready for a relationship?

We find the girls still speaking about Angela's "love life". In response to Janet's advice, Angela replies, "I've heard what you've had to say and I think I like him a little, however I am still trying to deal with the shock of it all".

Angela further explains how she felt overwhelmed and scared when Emmanuel initially revealed his feelings towards her. "Guys, he told me that before he met me, he had a missing rib, just like Adam. However after spending time together, he felt that I was his missing rib". The two girls try as hard as they can to keep straight faces, however they fail miserably and they burst into laughter.

"Christian guys these days have some serious chat up lines", retorts Janet, "what next, I wonder?"

Jokingly, Kemi adds, "I wonder if every time he reads Philippians 4 v 8, he thinks of you". Angela looks on as the two girls laugh among themselves. Keeping a half straight face, Angela adds, "What he said to me is the stuff that goes into the speech just before the proposal, not from someone you barely know".

However, in Emmanuel's defence, Angela explains that, although his approach was a bit strange, "He is a really great guy". She adds, "He always listens to me and offers me advice whenever I go through something. He is also great company, I can spend a whole day with him, and it will seem like just a few hours: but I appreciate him as just a friend and nothing more."

Kemi and Janet are convinced that Angela is in denial about her feelings towards Emmanuel. They believe that deep inside, she is interested in him. Their suspicions are confirmed a bit later on when Angela asks, "How do you know if you are ready for a relationship?"

(To be continued)

What would Joseph do?

We return to the love story between Jacob and Rachael recorded in Genesis 29. Rachael took Jacob to her father's village. After staying there for about a month, Genesis 29 v 15 says, "Laban said to him, 'You shouldn't work for me without pay just because we are relatives. Tell me how much your wages should be." Verse 18 contains Jacob's response, "Since Jacob was in love with Rachael, he told her father, I'll work for you for seven years if you'll give me Rachael, your younger daughter, as my wife."

In the end both parties agreed, and in Genesis 29 v 20 we read, "So Jacob worked seven years to pay for Rachael. But his love for her was so strong that it seemed to him but a few days."

A relationship where both individuals involved are at the same uni has different implications to a relationship where they are not at the same uni. This is because, in the former, both individuals are tied to a particular location, whereas in the latter, there is freedom of movement for one or both individuals in the relationship. In the former, you are mostly likely going to be in each other's faces constantly, whereas in the latter, you may only get to see the other person occasionally. Clearly both cases have their downsides as well as positives.

What makes the former case particularly challenging is that every day is a test. Every interaction is an opportunity for either building each other up or hurting each other.

In view of the prospect of facing such a challenge on an almost daily basis, considerable thought has to go into whether you are ready to enter into a relationship or not. Your partner is most likely going to be your second greatest source of strength, second to God, whilst simultaneously being your second greatest source of frustration, second only to yourself.

How inspiring is the love story between Jacob and Rachael? He too was tied down to a single location: Laban's village. Initially he was there for seven years; for the majority of students a degree is on average three years.

The Bible says that his love for Rachael made him even more patient. I am sure they were not without times of difficulty, but they persevered. Below is a poem, inspired by the love story between Jacob and Rachael.

In asking whether you are ready for a relationship, ask yourself, "Do I have a timely concept of love?"

A timely concept of Love

Love takes time
And time gives love a chance to grow.
Time and love are the perfect couple
They both give and take and take to give.
One completes the other
Once they join together as one, as husband with wife
They give birth to a sense of urgency.
Suddenly. A year becomes a month, and a month becomes a week
And a week becomes a day, until minutes become seconds.
Or
A book becomes a chapter, and a chapter becomes a paragraph
And a paragraph becomes a sentence until words become letters.
Jacob was a man, whose love for Rachael stood the test of time
Genesis 29v20 says, "He waited seven years for her
But they seemed like a few days to him because of his great love for her"
Christ longs to be, reunited with His bride to be
Behold I come quickly He says
A 1000 years is like a day in God's eyes,
The Lord is not slow in keeping His promises
For the sake of Love, let us pray that we change our concept of what true love is
Because true love, truly is Patient.

Experiment

- Have a plan for the relationship and make sure you question your intentions.

- By now you should be thinking about getting an accountability figure involved, to help deal with the issues that arise in the relationship.

- When you start to feel that the relationship is becoming more important than it should, then prayerfully consider practical actions you can take to help put the relationship in its rightful place.

CHAPTER 13

More than friends at uni

In a press release by the UNITE-Group, it was stated that "going to university could even increase your chances of tying the knot. One in five (20%) former students are married or in a long term relationship with their uni love." Prince William and Kate followed the trend by beginning their love story at the University of St Andrews. We've all heard it said that you may find your spouse at uni, or at the very least, some life-long friends.

For some, finding a "special someone" may play a significant part in the decision to go to uni. Subsequently this may become a distraction. Whilst researching for this book I came across a phenomenon in America dubbed "Ring by Spring".

According to an article written by Ashley McIlwain, entitled "Ring by Spring", she describes the phenomenon as one characterised by "young Christian singles eagerly seeking out a spouse at Christian universities everywhere." She adds that the goal is to get an engagement ring by spring, before the end of the academic year.

It is unclear whether the phenomenon is driven by desire to simply have the "Big Dream Wedding" or because the students involved want to honour God, in accordance with 1 Corinthians 7 v 9. However one thing that remains clear is that it is important to avoid awakening love until it right time (Song of Solomon 2 v 8). Nowhere is this truer than at uni.

The difference between Conversion and Baptism

When a person initially gives their life to God, God begins working on the person's heart. A change, invisible to the physical eye occurs as the person receives a new nature. However, in the absence of a public declaration of this inward conversion, people may remain unaware of the conversion, at least in the early stages. When a person gets baptised, however, a public declaration is made of their faith in God.

Relationships follow a similar pattern. In the initial stages of the relationship, where we have friends who like each other, we have an 'inward conversion'. This is where both partners acknowledge that they have mutual feelings for each other. At this stage, it may not be visible that a relationship is about to start. Similarly when Paul got converted, in Acts 9 v26b, believers 'did not believe that he had truly become a believer'.

It is important then, that when 'friends who like each other' become 'more than friends', a public declaration of an inward conversion occurs. My Pastor always says that 'The devil works in the dark'. Therefore it is our duty as Christians to avoid walking in the dark and hiding behind the shadows of pride. It is important that we bring the now flourishing relationship before the attention of a spiritually mature accountability figure. Doing this shows that you care a lot about the relationship and about the other person.

In terms of spreading the 'good news' about your relationship, you should tell your circle of close friends. At the same time, give them the command to preach the 'good news', as it were. This is the most natural way, as it avoids the awkward comments that can easily show up on social media platforms.

Accountability

I sincerely believe that if you truly care about the other person, you will seek ways protect the innocence of the relationship. The best way to do this is through accountability. Without accountability, your conscience is more likely to get suffocated under the pressure of youthful desires. It may be hard to view things from a wider perspective. You are more likely to "get away with certain things", but this is likely to harm the innocence of the friendship.

When considering accountability, you may feel somewhat vulnerable. Hence it is ideal to confide in someone older, with experience. Making yourself accountable to your peers is more likely to generate gossip than progress.

There are other reasons that people fail to seek accountability:

- Pride – I can do this by myself.
- To avoid vulnerability – I don't want to be judged.
- Fear – I don't want to be taken advantage of.

In response to the first reason, 1 Peter 5v7 says to humble yourself before God, as God gives more grace to the humble but resists the prideful. In response to the second reason, seek someone who is truly spiritual and who will "restore you gently", according to Galatians 6v1. Lastly, in response to the third reason, confide in someone you trust.

Benefits of accountability:

- Helps protect the innocence of the relationship
- Gives you hope – especially from someone with experience
- Encourages self-discipline

Moreover, there is tremendous strength to resist temptation when there are more than two people. The Bible says "two may not be strong enough, but a cord of three strands may be strong enough" (Ecclesiastes 4v2).

Really pray about to whom to become accountable. It is a big decision, because it will only work if you are totally honest with the person. This requires a high level of trust. Hence serious prayer is required.

Observation

Uni is a battlefield for purity. Researchers at the University of Southampton, in a survey, found that the average time between a young person's first kiss and losing their virginity was 3.2 years, about the average length of a degree. The social scientists at the OSE, point towards the lack of supervision and accountability, together with youthful desires, as the leading factors.

Innocence of a relationship

After watching the movie, it seems that Kemi has a lot on her mind. This is evidenced by her question, "What do you guys think about kissing?" Immediately, Angela responds by expressing her view that, "as much as possible it should be avoided", as her older sister had advised her that it would lead to "other things".

Similarly Janet, through her experiences in being in a relationship with her boyfriend, shares the same sentiment. She adds, "As best you can, try and delay physical intimacy for as long as possible, instead focus on the friendship aspect of the relationship".

In response to what the girls have to say, Kemi pours out her heart about her dilemma: "You see the guy upstairs, I really had a thing for him. I thought he looked good. Initially, he wasn't interested in me, but after one rave a few months ago, we managed to exchange numbers. One of the reasons why I came to uni was to find a new man, not just a typical 'Yo!

Yo! Guy'. The guy upstairs seemed like a good guy, he was everything I was looking for in a guy.

It was after we shared our first kiss that I started to release that he was after one thing. It seemed like all he was interested in was getting me into his bed. Things started moving too fast for my liking, but he promised me that he wouldn't take things that far. I stopped believing him when he started asking me to act out his fantasies."

Janet and Angela plead with Kemi to end whatever is going on between her and the guy upstairs. "There is no real friendship between you, so there is no basis for a relationship, let alone what he is asking you to do", says Janet. In agreement, Angela adds, 'He hasn't put a ring on your finger, girl'.

What would Joseph do?

It is safe to assume that the population surveyed by the researchers at the University of Southampton was mainly comprised of Non-Christians. Therefore the findings should come as no surprise.

However, such findings are equally likely to occur in relationships were Christians are unequally yoked with Non-Christians (2 Corinthians 6v14). Moreover, this can also be applied to relationships were both parties are Christians. With regards to the first case, being intimate with someone who does not share the same value system as you will eventually lead to compromise in order to please the other party.

With regards to the second case, it is important to realise that the battle is not won by the strong. The battle for purity is won by those who realise that their flesh is weak and thus take the necessary precautions to avoid any form of compromise.

A friend of mine – an amazing guy too – always makes sure that if he is having female company over, another guy is present. Not that he thinks anything will happen, but just so that wisdom's cry (Proverbs 1) is not ignored. If we, as God's children, at uni had this mindset, we would avoid many of the temptations which serve to frustrate our souls.

The problem lies in underestimating the power of youthful desires. We fail when we fail to flee. This is not something you need to experience in order to believe. The Bible is God's word. As God, He knows what makes us tick, so take His word for it.

Let's face it, humans desire to connect with each other at one level or another. Even Jesus had desires; I can imagine Him desiring a family of His own. Desires are not necessarily evil. They can be good or bad. Desires are what make us human. However they also leave us vulnerable to temptation.

Jesus had desires and I believe that was the only reason the devil was able to tempt him. However, his desires were pure, as "he faced all of the same testings we do, yet He did not sin" (Hebrews 4v15).

In addressing the issue of the rampant sexual immorality within the church in Corinth, the Apostle Paul advised the church to 'run from sexual sin!' and not even put up a fight (1 Corinthians 6v18). It seemed he was well aware of the power of lust and youthful desires, especially among young adults.

Notice that the Apostle Paul doesn't say you should fast and pray. Don't get me wrong, fasting and praying are very powerful weapons we have as Christians. However, his instructions are that 'each man should have his own wife, and each woman should have her own husband' (1 Corinthians 7v2). A little later we read that 'It's better to marry than to burn with lust' (1 Corinthians 7v9b). The message is clear and yet so often overlooked.

According to Ted Cunningham, a proponent of young marriages and the author of the book "Young and in Love", states that "Saying 'let's wait' is easier when 'I do' is not far away." The author outlines the steps to creating a life-long relationship for young adults. He also refutes the arguments made against young marriages. This is a must-read for anyone serious about honouring God with their relationship, especially at this stage in life.

Experiment

The Bible says not to be ignorant of the enemy's weapons. If you can see a certain pattern of behaviour, then look at ways of interrupting the chain of cause and effect. Otherwise, ignorance can lead to problems.

The devil works in the dark, so do everything in the light. Make sure an accountability figure is kept informed about the relationship and its progress. Moreover, spread the good news about your relationship to your close friends, this will help keep it fruitful.

Start reading books that encourage godly relationships.

PART 5

Money Matters

CHAPTER 14

Money coming in at uni

Under the new reforms, tuition fees have roughly doubled and in some cases trebled from around £3300 per year to £6000 and £9000 respectively. In view of this, it is important to keep in mind that you do not have to pay anything upfront. This immediately debunks a few myths about the implications of the increase in tuition fees.

The most common myths, as detailed on factsonfees.com, are:

- I don't have £9000, so I can't go to uni
- Parents can't afford the fees
- The poor won't be able to go to uni

The reality is that, unless you are super-rich and can pay your tuition fees upfront, you do not have to pay anything until you are earning £21,000 per year, under the new reforms.

The majority of university students anticipate the day when student finance is reflected in their bank accounts. You would think they had won the lottery or something. 'Your student finance will be paid into your bank account tomorrow' is a universally celebrated text message by students of all walks of life.

However, in that moment of excitement, you need to be mindful of the proportion of the money that is freely given and the proportion of money that is borrowed. Furthermore, you should make a distinction between the proportion of money that is yours and the proportion of money that belongs to God, preferably in reverse order. Below are a few definitions that will help us make these distinctions.

Definitions

Tuition fee loan
This is defined by the department for Business Innovation & Skills (BIS) as a loan from the Government, used to cover the cost of higher education tuition. It is available to eligible students studying for their first degree. This means that you don't have to find the money to pay for tuition costs before or while you are studying and you don't have to start repaying the loan until you are earning over £21,000 a year.

Maintenance Loan
This is defined as a loan to help you with other costs associated with going to university, things like accommodation, food, travel and course materials. Be mindful of the fact that both the tuition fee loan and the maintenance loan will be combined into one when the time comes for you to repay the borrowed money. The amount you get is based on:

- Where you live and study
- Your household income
- How much non-repayable grant (previously called maintenance grant) you are entitled to.

Table 3.   *Amount of living cost loan you can get*

Circumstances	Amount*
Living away from home and studying in London	£7,675
Living away from home and studying outside London	£5,500
Living at your parent's home	£4,375
Studying abroad as part of your UK course	£5,895

The amount for each circumstance is correct at the time of writing

Non-repayable living cost grant

Formerly known as the maintenance grant, this falls under non-repayable financial help from the government. Eligible full-time students with a household income of £42,600 or less can obtain this. As the name suggests, this is money you don't have to pay back. This grant is worth up to £3,250.

The full grant of £3,250 will be awarded to full-time student with a household income of £25,000 or less. Partial non-repayable grants will be available if you have a household income of between £25,000 and £42,600.

In the tables that follow, we can see the kind of support on offer to students. The figures are based on household income.

Table 4.   *2012/13 Financial Support by Household Income – students living away from home and studying outside of London*

Household income	Living cost grant	Living cost loan	Total
£25,000 or less	£3,250	£3,875	£7,125
£30,000	£2,341	£4,330	£6,671
£35,000	£1,432	£4,784	£6,216
£40,000	£523	£5,239	£5,762
£45,000	0	£5,288	£5,288

For household income equal or greater that £45,000, the living cost grant is 0, whilst the living cost loan decreases in value.

Table 5.   *2012/13 Financial Support by Household Income – students living away from home and studying in London*

Household income	Living cost grant	Living cost loan	Total
£25,000 or less	£3,250	£6,050	£9,300
£30,000	£2,341	£6,505	£8,846
£35,000	£1,432	£6,959	£8,391
£40,000	£523	£7,414	£7,937
£45,000	0	£7,463	£7,463

For household income equal or greater that £45,000, the living cost grant is 0, whilst the living cost loan decreases in value.

Bursary

these are also non-repayable funds which can be as much as £1,500. This is given on top of any support provided by the government. The precise details depend on each university. Generally speaking, to be eligible you may be asked to meet the following, among other things;

- UK student
- Full time student
- EU students may also be eligible
- Low household income (£25,000)
- Meet conditions of the university's offer

Biblical Economics

Having looked at what kind of funding is available, it is now possible to make a distinction between money that is given to you freely and money that you borrow. Clearly, the former includes living cost grants and bursaries. The latter includes tuition fee loans and living cost loans. With this in mind we can now address the issue of tithing.

When you think of tithing, you immediately think of Malachi 3v8-10, where it says, "Should people cheat God? Yet you have cheated me! "But you ask, "What do you mean? When did we ever cheat you?" "You have cheated me of the tithes and offerings due to me." It is important as Christians to honour God with our finances. It will not go unnoticed, as God promises to open the windows of heaven and pour out His blessings upon us.

It can be argued that the majority of students do not work; therefore some may think that this exempts them from the obligation to tithe. However, in making a distinction between non-repayable and repayable funding, we discovered that the former belongs to us, whereas the latter has to return to the government in the future.

Therefore, apart from repayable loans, or interest free overdraft allowances, we should be tithing money from our grants, bursaries, scholarships and other extra funding we may get in the process, which is non-repayable. Not only that, but we have to make it a priority.

Testimonies

Damy, BA Law

The saying, "with God all things are possible", is the core statement of my testimony. On the 4th of October, I found out that the student loans company were not going to fund me for my final year at university, which meant that I would have to raise more than £7,500 in order to stay at university.

Thank God for blessing me with an amazing mother, because she decided that she would fund my education. However, the lawyer in me decided that I would fight this issue with the student loans company. I had a great amount of faith in God; I was counting every situation with joy. However, along the way my joy was tarnished by my flesh and I let the situation decide my destination.

I was hurt and my faith was destroyed by the thoughts in my head. I could not function properly, I became fragile and depressed; I was a prisoner within my own emotions, with panic attacks, headaches, and stomach aches - you name it, I had it! It wasn't too long until I went into a state of depression. I would cry without a reason, I felt my heart breaking, but I could not ask for healing, because I drifted away from God.

I was surrounded by people, but all I saw was loneliness. I had exchanged the word of God that gave me courage, hope and peace, for a voice with doubt, sorrow and hopelessness. Thank God for a prayerful family and friends, because without their prayers you would have been reading my grave stone, not my testimony.

One morning in the middle of a new month, I woke up and was tired of being lonely. I started to remember where God had taken me, how difficult the road had been and, more importantly, the testimony I had behind those trials and tribulation. So, I told my soul to arise, I started to lean on the feet of my master, I asked for forgiveness and I started to pray towards my loan. But still I had no faith.

Over time I became a pest to student loan officers. I would call every day and say, "Sorry to disturb you, but I just wanted to see if there was progress in my case". They always replied, "Ms Alade, like we have said plenty of times, we are not funding you for this academic year and the decision still stands. There is no way we are over turning that decision".

I was tired and frustrated, until I heard the voice of God; He told me that I would receive my loan and that the situation will be sorted out. I was so happy, I called in and heard a cold voice from student loan saying,

"No, Ms Alade we are not over turning our decision." I was angry at God; I thought maybe I heard wrong or I was being teased, so I stopped bothering the student loan company and I accepted my situation.

Meanwhile, I was told that was a conference going on at my church back home. At first, I hesitated, as I didn't want to go. However, something inside me pushed me to go, and thank God I went, as that's where God provided me with my breakthrough.

The pastor asked us to sing a song if we were having trouble and I decide to put the student loan within the lines of the song. A few days after the conference God told me to call the student loans company and so I did! This phone call was with a different student loan officer, who calmly said, "Oh Ms Alade things have been sorted out and we are funding you for the academic year. The money will be in your account shortly".

I thought to myself that God is good, but I was ashamed that I lost faith when I should have been still and known that He is God.

Extra Funding At Uni

Access to Learning funds

This is a discretionary fund administered by universities and colleges which can provide help for students in financial difficulties who may need extra financial support to stay in higher education.

Disabled Students' Allowances (DSAs)

Available to help you if you are doing a higher education course and will incur extra costs because of a disability (including a long-term health condition, mental health condition or specific learning difficulty such as dyslexia). DSAs are paid in addition to the standard student finance package and are available if you are studying on a full-time, full-time distance learning or part time course. They are not dependant on income and do not have to be repaid.

Educational Grants Advisory Service (EGAS)

EGAS hold a database of charitable organisations offering educational grants and loans to students studying in the UK: *www.family-action.org.uk*

Part-time employment

You can search for vacancies on campus, for example in the student union. You can also apply for jobs around your local area and the Careers Centre will be able to help you find part-time employment. It is generally advised not to work more than 15 hours per week during term time.

Which Bank To Join?

This is an important consideration, especially as you'll need to have an account, preferably a student account, with a bank or building society in order to receive any funding for your studies. With so many banks around, it can be difficult to choose the right one for you.

The best advice I can give is not to get misled by enticing freebies. A large overdraft facility is worth more than free giveaways. You should aim to join a bank which will offer you the largest interest free overdraft facility, as this will be useful when unexpected bills or fines come through the post.

Table 6.   *High street banks offering an interest free overdraft facility*

Banks	Amount			
	£500	£1000	£1500	£2000
Santander		1st year	3rd year	4+ years
Halifax	Up to £3000 (depends on financial status at time of application)			
NatWest		1st year	3rd year	5+ years
HSBC	Up to £3000 (depends on financial status and usage of the account)			
Lloyds TSB	6 months	7-9 months	10+ months	4+ years
Barclays	Up to £2000 (depends on financial status at time of application)			

Notes

- Banks will give you a student account if it is recognised as your main account. This will be the account that your student finance will go into, among other things.

- As a direct result of the above, you cannot have more than one student accounts.

- HSBC, Santander and Halifax offer you interest on positive balances in your student account. However, research these banks as they pay interest differently.

- HSBC have a student bursary competition, where eight fortunate students can win £15,000 to help them as they enter Higher Education.

CHAPTER 15

Money going out at uni

The rise in tuition fees means that students starting university in September 2012 or later should, according to the Guardian, 'expect to finish their degree with debts approaching £60,000'. This is a huge contrast to those who started studying in 2008, who by the time they graduated, left with debts totalling around £22,000.

Given the tripling of student debt, it is now more essential to be shrewd with our expenditures. In particular, it is important to have a practical attitude when it comes to managing the amount of debt we get into as students. It is easy to think that, as long as the money coming in at uni is greater than the money going out, then we should be financially ok.

However, as we saw in the previous chapter, from the money we get from student finance, a proportion of it is freely given, whereas the rest is borrowed and has to be returned. Moreover, the 'free money' from an overdraft facility also has to be returned one day. Therefore it is important that we are shrewd with the amount of money going out at uni.

There is a real danger for students, when compared to non-students, to become very complacent with their expenditure. In view of the interest free student overdraft facility, students part with their money more comfortably then their non-student peers, relying on this financial cushion. In contrast, non-students have no such privileges, or at least not to the same extent. The average interest free overdraft facility for non-students (current account) is around £300. Anything above the overdraft limit will result in high interest rate charges. As a result, non-students have to be more disciplined in their spending.

Money Management

There are various ways in which students can be shrewd with their expenditures. However this requires a bit of effort and more thought over and above what is required when mindlessly using the *'free money'* to Spend! Spend! Spend! That said, the little that is required here, can pay off huge dividends; better yet, it can save you hundreds of pounds. Below is a list of some of the ways in which you can manage your expenditure better.

Utilise your local Charity shop

When it comes to buying consumer electricals such as TVs or Microwaves, buying these items in a charity shop can drastically reduce your spending. It is quite possible to find a fully working 28 inch TV for around £10 in a charity shop. For me, this beats buying a 28 inch plasma screen TV from the high street for over ten times as much.

Avoid unnecessary library fines

It is important to keep a record of when your books are due - usually you will get email notification. Returning library books may at times seem like a hassle, especially when it involves trying to figure out where you last saw the overdue copy. However acting promptly will save you having to pay large fines, especially if the book is borrowed on a short loan basis.

Fill in the HC1 form

Most NHS treatments are free, although there can be charges for some things. You can get help with NHS health costs such as:

- NHS Prescriptions (where these are not free)
- NHS Dental treatment, including check-ups (where these are not free)
- Sight Tests (where these are not free).

Students who are eligible for free treatments fall into the following groups.

- Under 19 and still in full-time education.
- Holder of a valid NHS Exemption Certificate (HC2 form, which can be obtained by filling in a HC1 form). HC1 forms can be obtained from your uni's student support office.

Please note that both the NHS treatments and eligibility criteria outlined above are not exhaustive; for a comprehensive list please visit direct-gov.co.uk. Had I known about the HC1 form, I would have saved over £200 in NHS treatments whilst at uni.

Get a student railcard

This is really good, especially for those whose uni is quite a distance away from home. At just £28 for a whole year, you can literally save a fortune on rail tickets when going home over the holiday or taking trips across England. You can also get a three year student railcard at £65, which saves you having to renew your one year railcard over and over again. To be eligible you need:

- To be aged 16-25 or a full time student
- Valid passport or UK driving licence

For more information please visit; *www.16-25railcard.co.uk*

Have you got the right phone contract?

Phone bills can be very volatile over time, especially if you are on a contract. Given that most, if not all, the monthly contracts that I've come across are uncapped, it is not surprising to find yourself paying out lots more than required by the contract.

This is because we unwittingly exceed the amount of minutes, texts or data usage permitted by the contract, without being informed by the service providers. Gone are the days where you would receive a text saying that you are about to go over your allowance.

Nowadays, unless you keep track of your usage, you are likely to go over and face very high charges for any minutes, texts and data used outside the tariff plan. Based on rough calculations, I paid out more than one and a half times, on average - under my two year contract - than I meant to. Service providers love customers like me, who are just too busy to keep track of their monthly usage.

There are a couple of options available to avoid such wastage;

Capped tariff plans

Different service providers can offer tariff plans which are capped. However unless you ask, they don't usually make you aware of these.

Avoid calling non-geographic numbers with your mobile phone

That is, numbers that do not begin with 01, 02, and 03. A few examples of non-geographic numbers are those that start with 0843, 0844, 0845, 0870, 0871, 0872, etc. They cost considerably more than standard calls, especially from mobile phones. To avoid these non-geographic numbers, 'Saynoto0870.com' is a great website designed to help you find alternative numbers for companies that use them.

Billmonitor.com

This is a great website founded by mathematicians in Oxford. It analyses your online mobile phone bill and, through the use of a mobile price comparison calculator, recommends a better deal for you. It is easy to use and can help you save lots.

Contracts

In today's competitive climate, it is not surprising to find numerous contracts of differing lengths aimed at different groups of people, across a broad range of services. More importantly, no longer do nine month contracts, for example, end automatically after the specified period. It is far more likely that the nine month contract is made on a rolling basis. That is, although it is only after the specified period that can you cancel the contract, it doesn't mean that the contract ends in nine months.

Service providers usually ask that you notify them about cancelling a contract at least a month before the contract is meant to end. Speaking from experience, failure to do this can prove to be an expensive mistake.

Contracts also have binding power. This is fairly obvious, but easy to forget in practice; again this can prove to be an expensive mistake. It is important to convince yourself of the necessity of obtaining a particular service. Gym memberships, for example, have to be paid regardless of whether or not you use the gym, as long as you have signed the contract. I could have saved myself a lot of money if I had simply looked at whether or not I would consistently use the gym. Unfortunately for me; I didn't.

Groceries

When you've been in the supermarket three times in a single day you know you're in trouble. These are the confessions of a student shopaholic. It is common among students to find groceries to be among their highest expenditures – probably second only to rent. However, unlike rent, the cost of groceries can fluctuate. This makes food shopping extremely important to monitor.

There numerous websites which can help you manage the amount of money you spend on groceries, through the use of meal plans. For example, the Resourcefulcook.com is a great website, designed to help you cut costs, as well as reduce the amount of food wasted. It does this through carefully arranged meal plans which take into account your lifestyle (diet, budget, and the kind of store cupboard you have).

This is ideal for students, as it can potentially save you hundreds over the university journey. Given that variety is the spice of life, this too is an added benefit of the meal plans, as they encourage cooking that goes beyond bangers and mash.

Shopping for Daniel Fast

The cost of groceries during the fast, will be considerably higher in comparison to standard groceries. Make sure you consider this before starting the fast. Below are two tables which are designed to help you decide what to buy, and what not to buy, during the fast.

Table 7.   *List of foods to buy under Daniel Fast*

Shopping Basket			
	Breakfast	Snacks	Main meal
All vegetables	100% vegetable soup100% vegetable juice	Hummus	Potatoes, sweet potatoes, peppers, tomatoes, onions.
All legumes			Kidney beans, butter beans, pinto bean, lentils
All whole grains	Oats, Wheatabix	Chapatti, flatbread, rice cakes.	Brown rice, whole-wheat pasta, couscous.

Shopping Basket			
	Breakfast	Snacks	Main meal
Fruits	100% fruit juices	All fruits	All fruits
Nuts & Seeds	All nuts	Popcorn, All nuts	All nuts
Soya products	Soya milk	Roasted soya beans	Soya mince
Dairy replacement	Oat milk, Rice milk, and Soya milk		

Table 8.   *List of foods to avoid under Daniel Fast*

Animal products	Beef, lamb, pork, poultry, and fish.
Dairy products	Milk, cheese, cream, butter, and eggs
Sweeteners	Sugar, honey, syrups, sweetener
Breads	Goods which use yeast should be avoided
Refined/processed foods	Artificial flavourings, food additives, artificial preservatives, and goods made from concentrate.
Fats	Butter, margarine, and foods high in fat, especially deep fried foods
Drinks	Coffee, tea, herbal teas, soft drinks, energy drinks, and alcohol.

PART 6

Maximising Potential

CHAPTER 16

God's University Guide

Questions have been raised as to whether 'students have the interest, energy or expertise to meaningfully interrogate the data included in league tables", as stated in the Higher Education Funding Council of England report (2008). With this in mind, I conducted a study titled "How reliable are university league tables in the UK?"

League tables play an important role, as prospective students sift through all the universities within the UK in search for the right one. According to the UNITE report (2007), in response to the question, "Which of these were important to you in your selection of university", 29% of 1600 respondents said; "university league tables".

With this in mind, it is important therefore, that league tables are reliable so that students can make choices based on reliable information. However, there have been many criticisms made against league tables. For example, they don't include many crucial factors; e.g. location, distance from home, living costs, bursaries and other financial support. That said, it would be more or less impossible for a league table to factor in "distance from home", for example.

Table 9. *The variables included across the 2012 league tables*

Variables	Times	Sunday Times	Guardian
Student Satisfaction	✓	✓	
Research Quality	✓	✓	
Entry Standards	✓		✓
Student: Staff Ratio	✓	✓	✓
Services & Facilities Spend	✓		✓
Firsts/2:1s Awarded	✓	✓	
Graduate Prospects	✓	✓	
Completion	✓	✓	✓
NSS Teaching quality		✓	✓
NSS Feedback			✓
NSS Overall Satisfaction			✓
Value added			✓
Peer Assessment		✓	

The study examined recent editions of the three most popular league tables which are The Times, The Sunday Times, and The Guardian. The approach taken in order to find out whether or not the league tables were reliable, was to assess whether the variables included in each league table were measuring the same thing: that is quality. Using a statistical method called *factor analysis*, the results showed that this was the case.

Therefore the results didn't provide strong enough evidence to conclude that league tables are unreliable. However, relatively speaking, the results showed that The Times league table was the most reliable, closely followed by The Sunday Times. The Guardian, although still reliable, was regarded to be the least reliable of the three league tables.

Statistically reliable but biased?

There is evidence to suggest that league tables, although reliable, may be biased towards certain universities. In order to provide evidence for this, the data included in the most reliable league table under our analysis - the Times 2012, will be rearranged. In doing this, we will avoid giving each university a total aggregate score, which is the current practice; rather each university will be given a dominant quality.

A dominant quality is the most common quality a university receives across all its variables. For each variable, a university will be awarded a quality that ranges from outstanding to poor. In order to achieve this, we rearrange the values for each variable, from best to worst.

Given that there are eight variables; where four or more variables are of the same quality we conclude that, whatever quality they are, is the dominant quality. Furthermore, where there is uncertainty about the dominant quality, we will take the average dominant quality.

Appendix A shows the modified Times league table, which takes into account the dominant quality of universities. The table suggests that there are 16 universities which the Times league table is either biased towards or against. This finding is true, given that we assume that each variable is given equal importance (equal weights). After all, whose is to say one variable is more important than the other?

Looking closely at the results we see that The Times league table is biased towards Sussex University. According to our Dominant Quality league table, it has a dominant quality of above average. However it is ranked 14th in The Times league table and is placed above Edinburgh, Nottingham and Sheffield, which all have a dominant quality of outstanding.

Moreover The Times league table is biased against Kings College London and Newcastle University. The Dominant Quality league table suggests that they should be in the top group. Lower down the league table, we find similar results. For example, Brunel is also under-ranked, whereas universities such as Bangor, Northumbria and Central Lancashire are all over-ranked.

Testimonies

Tino, BSc Economics

I had my heart set on going to Birmingham University. At the time, it was ranked 4th for economics in the Guardian League table. This was a very important factor for me, at that time, as I believed it would look good on my CV. I got ahead of myself, as I told one my friends who lived in Birmingham, that I was coming to study there.

The grade requirement was ABB, which I felt I could achieve, however my predicted grades said otherwise. But I still thought to myself, "they will still consider me."

It was as if I had based my whole future in going to Birmingham University. I never saw myself going to the other universities, which I had to pick out of necessity, let alone the uni that I actually ended up going to.

I can remember the day that I discovered that the university had responded to my application. I was cautiously optimistic. Whenever I find myself in these type of situations, be it a job application, grant application, or even a business proposal, I always skim read to find words such as "unfortunately" or "we are sorry", before actually reading the entire reply. I do this to get rid of the suspense as quickly as possible.

As I read the email, I found those dreaded words, as if engraved in the letter. I quickly thought to myself, "impossible, how could they not accept me?" I couldn't believe it, I had my future all planned out, or so I thought.

I took a few days to get over the disappointment. However, I began to encourage myself with the words, "I am going to see success as God sees success". It was easier said than done, however, as I write this book, I can truly say that God has given me more success than I could have ever asked for.

A few weeks went by, and I had received no further replies from the remaining universities. I remember being encouraged by my Law teacher to reconsider one of the universities on my list. However, the deadline for making changes to the choice of universities was fast approaching.

It wasn't until one day in a local library, that I felt God leading me to consider another university. I found myself looking through several prospectuses shelved beside each other. However there was one, in particular, that stood out to me. It was the University of Essex prospectus. I wasn't just the colour that caught my eye, but just everything about it, from the course description to a brief description of its facilities.

It was then that I felt that the University of Essex was the right place for me. However, by this time, the deadline for making changes to the choice of universities had passed. This didn't deter me however. So, with the help of my then-form tutor, I was able to change my choice of university for Essex. It really felt like a God moment.

Patience, BA Accounting and management

I went from pursuing fashion to physiotherapy, then ended up doing accountancy. When I applied for physiotherapy, I managed to secure two out of my five choices. However, I was declined from my first choice: Birmingham University.

Around the same time, I managed to gain some work experience through the NHS. It was a two day placement, as a physiotherapist. It was then that I began to question whether I wanted to spend £12,000 studying physiotherapy. After much thought, I realised that I was making the wrong choice.

I ended up declining both my offers and applied for accountancy and management at Aston University. Fortunately, they gave me a conditional offer. However, in the end I did not meet their requirements. At that stage I was quite upset. Not only had I rejected both my offers for physiotherapy, but now I had been rejected by Aston University as well.

I was determined not to give up, so as the clearing stage approached, I was determined to get into my original first choices (Birmingham and Aston). I strongly believed that I was a worthy candidate for universities.

In the end I managed to get into Birmingham University, but on a different course. I had hoped that I would then be able to change course and enrol onto the accountancy course. However, once I arrived there, I wasn't unable to. So, for a year, I was stuck on a course I didn't want to do. I wanted to drop-out on several occasions, but my parents were so eager for me to stay. Looking back now, I can say that – that year benefited me, as it geared me up for what was to come.

With my on-going determination to study accountancy, I applied again. However, this time, I was fortunate enough to be offered an unconditional offer at the University of Essex.

Since being at Essex, so many doors have been opened for me. I have been involved in various societies, which have been the vehicle of numerous networking and personal development opportunities. I have also taken on various roles of management and leadership. Furthermore, being in an environment of like-minded people, one of my greatest accomplishments at Essex University has been the building up of my faith as a Christian, particularly through the Christian society – Jesus Alive Fellowship – which has also allowed me to be an encouragement to others. It has definitely led to maturity in every aspect of my life and accounts for a great amount of my personal development.

Jessica, BA Economics with French

While applying for University places during my A-levels, I had my mind set on studying at the University of Birmingham. As far as I was concerned, there was no reason why I wouldn't get in. Despite being able to choose five potential universities in my UCAS application I was very reluctant to fill all of them.

In my initial application, I only used up three of my five potential choices. My predicted grades were AAB, while the grade requirements to study my chosen course at Birmingham were ABB. Clearly my predicted grades exceeded the minimum requirement.

Furthermore, my personal statement looked impressive, or so I thought. I also had a good reference from my teacher and had previously done a lot of work experience which supported my application. I had planned my whole life around the University of Birmingham, from my accommodation to my future career prospects. I had already made plans with a friend of mine to potentially move in together.

At the time, my college offered 'UCAS sessions' with the Careers Department, where your University choices were discussed with a member of staff within the department. It was during one of these sessions, that a member of staff was able to persuade me to use up my five choices. She insisted, "You just never know what could go wrong! I have seen it too many times before; it's not random that you're given five choices, make use of them!" She then searched for my course on UCAS and suggested that I apply to Kingston and Essex – two Universities that I had never considered.

It was very wise of her, as I ended up being rejected for most of my University choices; including Birmingham, but was accepted at Kingston and Essex. Accident or design, you be the judge. But how unreal was that?

I was devastated and so I called up the different universities who rejected my application asking for further explanations. It did not make sense to me, as my predicted grades exceeded the grade requirements. I was even willing to change my course altogether in order to be given a place at the University of Birmingham. They did just that, but I knew that I was compromising, as I was unfamiliar with the course they offered.

What shocked me the most was their reason for not taking me. I had applied to study for a degree in Economics with French, even though I am a French native speaker. Apparently the course was not designed for 'native speakers'. Nonetheless, I was accepted at both Kingston and Essex for the same course. In the end, I decided to make Essex my firm choice and Kingston my second choice.

Despite not having done as well as I had hoped, as I missed the grade requirements by 40 UCAS points, Essex still offered me a place. I truly believe it was planned and directed by God, as studying at the University of Essex has given me some of the greatest years in my life. It has really moulded me into the young woman that I am today. I have learnt so much here, about myself, the people around me, about life and about God.

Lesson Learnt

As you can see, all three of us had our eyes set on one university. We can generalise this and call it "the ideal university", according to man. Some may say, "Oxford and Cambridge", others may say "the top 10 universities", still others may say the "Russell Groups of universities". However, what does God say about the ideal university? To play on Matthew 16 v 13-15 (NIV)

God had other plans for us. He knew that in coming to Essex we would thrive and produce much fruit. Looking back over my time at Essex, I sincerely believe that God has made me fruitful.

God knew that one day Jessica, Patience and I would take on the challenge to write a guide book to edify and educate the body of Christ. This book could have been written at the University of Birmingham, as we would have probably still met each other, although under different circumstances.

The next two chapters have been written by Jessica and Patience, respectively. This is evidence that, no matter which university you end up at, so long as God's blessing is on you, you will flourish. He knows what is best for us, and regardless of what a league table may say. It is best to listen to what God has to say.

CHAPTER 17

Why do students drop out of uni?

According to the annual figures from the Higher Education Statistics Agency (HESA), university drop-out rates have reached their highest level. As previously highlighted in chapter 3, lack of social integration is identified as one of the main reasons why some students drop out of uni. However, this is not the only reason; there are many other factors that we will uncover throughout this section.

Unsurprisingly, many prospective as well as current students are not aware of the factors which contribute to a students' decision to drop-out of university. Yet, being aware of potential causes of student drop-outs could potentially prevent people making the same mistakes, reduce the number of drop-outs and improve their overall university experience.

It is important that the term *'student drop-outs'* is formally defined. The Economist Gary S. Becker (1962) suggests two different definitions:

- **Leaving the college of registration** – that is, anyone that leaves the university to which they have been registered and then transfers elsewhere.

- **Not obtaining any qualifications whatsoever** – that is, those who fail to obtain a degree from any university.

For the purposes of this chapter, we will focus on the second definition. This is because the statistical evidence uses data which defines student drop-outs according to the second definition.

Furthermore, we must distinguish between *'Voluntary drop-out'* and *'Non-voluntary drop-out'*. The former is an individual's decision, out of choice, to withdraw themselves from a course of study, perhaps – for example - to enter employment. The latter is when the individual has no other choice but to withdraw from a course due to academic failure. In the context of this chapter we will focus on both elements.

Theories behind student dropouts: Rational Choice Theory

The term Rational Choice is defined by *Investopedia* as, "An economic principle that assumes that individuals always make prudent and logical decisions that provide them with the greatest benefit or satisfaction and that are in their highest self-interest". In other words, it suggests that individuals will always go for the options in life that pay back the most.

In the context of students at uni, there is a trade-off between the costs and the expected benefits of being at uni. We recommend that before setting off to uni, prospective students should make these calculations. According to Luke 14v28 (NIV), "suppose one of you wants to build a tower. Will he not first sit down and estimate the cost to see if he has enough money to complete it?" Doing so will help students assess whether going to uni is a beneficial investment or not.

In other words, will the expected benefits gained from the completion of their course exceed the costs of being at uni? If a student is 'rational', we should expect them to act on a decision that generates the highest level of benefits given their personal circumstances.

The main benefits of being at uni include the qualifications and skills students obtain over the course of their studies, as well as a strong network of friends. Moreover, there is a lot of evidence to suggest that future earnings increase with the amount of schooling. On the other hand, the costs of being at uni are tuition fees and the time spent studying, to name a few.

Student Time Allocation Problem

The student time allocation problem is another theory that can be used to explain why student dropout of uni. It was first developed by Becker (1965) and it carries the idea that students face a time allocation problem, where they trade-off between studying, leisure and sleep. It goes without saying that if students spend their time studying, they will most likely succeed in their exams, given that they work smart as well as work hard.

However, a balance is required between studying and leisure, as 'too much studying' not only makes jack a dull boy, but also prevents the necessary social integration that every student needs. Please refer to chapter 6 which contains numerous tips on time-saving techniques.

Similarly, there is a time constraint issue for students who choose to work during the term. By taking on employment, student may unwittingly increase their chances of dropping out, as less time may be devoted to studying. Thus, it is generally advised not to work more than 15 hours a week during term-time.

Statistical Evidence

We will now turn to the data provided by HESA. In analysing the data, we assessed the main factors which contributed to a student's decision to drop-out. We used an advanced statistical model *(Logistic Regression Model)* which helped us calculate the probability that a student would drop out, given his or her characteristics.

The data was collected from Full-time entrants in their first year, over a three year period (2006-2009). The different characteristics we looked at were student's age, gender, place of study (institution), qualifications prior to entry, social background and UCAS tariff points. In view of these characteristics, we calculated their probability of graduating. There were 11,000 students across 89 British Universities in our dataset.

Ten reasons why students decide to leave university

Without taking into account the characteristics of students, these are the ten reasons why students decide to leave uni, as identified by the HESA, in no particular order.

1   Successful completion of course

2   Academic Failure/left in bad standing/not permitted to progress

3   Transferred to another institution

4   Health reasons

5   Death

6   Financial reasons

7   Other personal reasons

8   Successful completion of course

9   Written off after lapse of time

10 Exclusion

Defining student characteristics

We are interested in how different characteristics affect a person's probability of dropping out. Below we define the different characteristics students can have, as outlined previously.

These are:

1   **Age** – it is based on the student's age at the point of entry. Those classed as 'Young' are aged 20 and below whilst those classed as 'Mature' are those aged 21 and above.

2   **Participation Neighbourhood** – This is divided into two groups (1) *Low Participation neighbourhood*: that is the number of young full-time first degree entrants each institution recruited from neighbourhoods with a low university participation rate. Another way to look at this is to view it as an indication of students that come from a lower social background (2) *Other participation neighbourhoods*: any neighbourhood that isn't part of the low participation neighbourhood.

3   **Institution Group** – 89 different universities have been grouped into five categories which are: (1) 1994 Group (2) Million Plus (3) Russell Group (4) University Alliance and (5) Other. A complete list of the different institutions which make up these groups can be found in the appendix section.

4   **Gender** – Either 'male' or 'female'

5   **Tariff Bands** – These are UCAS tariff scores obtained by entrants: (1) 80-119 (2) 180-239 (3) 300-359 (4) 420-479 (5) 540-998.

6   **Highest Qualification on Entry** – This is a measure of just how prepared students are in meeting the academic demands of university. It is also an indication of the resulting level of academic integration. This is because past performance has a bearing on factors, such as academic self-esteem, that determine your level of academic integration.

We focus on three types of types of qualifications, each of which carry a signal about the preparedness of each student. (1) 'A' level equivalent qualification implies that a student is fairly prepared (2) ONC or OND (including BTEC & SQA equivalents implies that a student is relatively not prepared (3) Baccalaureate qualification implies that a student is well prepared.

Findings

The findings from each calculation could only take on a value of between 0 and 1. This is the simple law of probability at work, where 1 implies certain and 0 implies impossible. Thus, the closer the result was to 1 the higher the probability that a student would graduate, given their characteristics. Conversely, a lower figure implied that a student was less likely to graduate, given their characteristics.

Table 10.   *Probability of graduating based on age (Qualification = **A levels**; Tariff = **420-279**)*

Age	Probability	Percentage
Mature	.720119	72%
Young	.621021	62%

The evidence suggests that mature students are more likely to graduate and thus less likely to drop out when compared to young students with 'A' Level qualifications, whose tariff scores are within the (420-479) band.

I suggest that mature students are less likely to drop out, as we can assume that they have a greater incentive to complete their course of study, because they are more likely to be grounded and thus wiser in managing other commitments. Moreover, being more mature, we can also assume that they can cope with the demands of being at university better.

In the same way, my study suggests that the qualifications obtained by students prior entry at university, also affect one's likelihood to dropout. As defined earlier, this has a lot do with how predisposed a student is to academic integration.

Table 11.   *Probability of graduating based on qualifications*

Qualifications	Probability	Percentage
'A' Level equivalent	.543494	54%
BTEC & SQA equivalents	.523596	52%
Baccalaureate	.811875	82%

Students with Baccalaureate qualifications are 82% likely to graduate; compared to 54% for 'A' Level holders and 52% for BTEC & SQA students. Those students with the highest level of qualifications; the Baccalaureate (well-prepared students) are less likely to drop-out when compared to those with lower qualifications; BTEC students (relatively non-prepared students).

However this does not mean that students with the lowest level of qualifications will never do better than those with higher levels of qualifications prior to matriculation. In chapter 5 we looked at myths about academic success, one of which was 'I have to be really clever to get a first'.

Although this evidence supports Tinto's theory about academic integration, that the higher your past performance, the more prepared you are and thus the more likely you are to graduate. However, even if you have had a bad academic record to date, you have God on your side. Through Christ, grace matters more than the grade, as we shall discover in the next chapter.

Table 12.   *Probability of graduating based on gender (Qualification = A levels; Tariff = 420-279)*

Gender	Probability	Percentage
Male	.631613	63%
Female	.642076	64%

Table 13. *Probability graduating based on gender (Qualification = A levels; Tariff = 540-998)*

Gender	Probability	Percentage
Male	.706796	70%
Female	.716084	71%

Males are more likely to drop-out in comparison to females across two bands of UCAS tariff scores. However, in both cases, the difference is very small. Unsurprisingly, students with higher UCAS tariffs (540-998) scores are less likely to drop-out than those with lower UCAS tariffs (420-479).

With regards to one's place of study (institutions), the level of student drop outs is more or less spread-out although out of five possible categories, which can be found in appendix B.

Table 14. *Probability of graduating based on Institutions (Qualification = A levels; Tariff = 420-479)*

Institutions groups	Probability	Percentage
1994 Group	.67148	67%
Million Plus	.64769	64%
Other	.62157	62%
Russell Group	.63912	63%

Table 15. *Probability of graduating based on Institutions (Qualification = Baccalaureate; Tariff =420-479)*

Institutions groups	Probability	Percentage
1994 Group	.84482	84%
Million Plus	.85608	86%
Other	.83758	83%
Russell Group	.85608	86%

Students with Baccalaureate qualifications and a tariff score between 420-479, who attend either a university within the '*Million Plus*' or the Russell group of universities have the highest probability of graduating (86%) when compared with the other listed groups of institutions.

Considering the fact that the majority of universities listed in the Russell group usually appear at the top of most university league tables, this suggests that there is a strong link between the quality of universities (league table ranking) and the quality of students – the top universities get the best students with the highest qualifications, and therefore show the lowest level of student drop outs.

Table 16.   *The Probability of graduating based on neighbourhood participation*

Participation Neighbourhood	Probability	Percentage
Lower Participation	.520464	52%
Other Participation	.463813	46%

With regards to the participation rate of neighbourhoods, a measure for social background, my finding demonstrate that those students who are from a lower participation neighbourhood are more likely to graduate and thus less likely to drop out in comparison to those are from 'other' participation neighbourhood.

I suggest that student from a lower social background have a lower drop out probability, as they have a bigger incentive to do well and graduate to hopefully better their current standard of living.

For the purpose of this book, I conclude by saying that the age of students is arguably the most significant factor which contributes to student drop outs, where mature students are less likely to drop out than young students. This is because they are better at coping with the demands of being at university. Therefore to increase the probability of graduating amongst young students, it is important that they have guidance throughout their course of study. This can be achieved by having mentors in their first year of university.

CHAPTER 18

Maximising your time at uni

University is an area of productive growth. You are not meant to just leave with a degree, but also with a full assurance that you have made the most of your time. An ideal goal for a successful individual would be to be 'bursting with experience' by the end of your three or more years at university.

For those who haven't had the best academic record, it can be all too easy to get caught up in the disappointment of previous academic failures. Grades, whether good or bad, should not be the 'be all and end all' of your university experience. In today's competitive world, high academic achievement is merely an aspect of what sets a student above the rest. For a lot of students, 'making the grade' can be an overwhelming factor; for others, it can be balanced by flawless experience.

I speak with first-hand knowledge and stand firm in my belief that grades should not be a barrier in any individual's journey. That said, I also believe that as a student, you should never minimise your efforts in achieving to the best of your ability. It is in your best interests to obtain grades that truly represent your ability.

You know yourself better than any lecturer, teacher or friend. You know what grades best represent your ability and it is important to realise the power within yourself to attain good grades.

Whether the grade is sweet or bitter, it would taste a whole lot sweeter with a healthy dose of experience.

Success is costly, but we can all afford it

I believe that there are students out there who are burning with the determination to prove to the academic admission staff that they made a wrong decision in refusing to offer them a place at the university. Still other students are left frustrated by top employers who recruit students mainly from universities that appear at the top of university league tables.

Individuals who fall into either one of these categories, may utter with frustration, 'where's the breakthrough in all of this?' You may feel that you have the licence to be frustrated and angry at the system, however let's not forget to ask ourselves, 'how can there be breakthrough without force?' The word force can be characterised by resilience, confidence, hard work, determination and perseverance.

Keeping a strong focus is a forceful element that will help you to attain your chosen aspirations. Understanding your purpose at university is essential; it provides you with discipline. Discipline in terms of creating a rewarding balance between your social and academic life. For students dealing with disappointment of failure, whether through unrepresentative grades or fruitless job hunting, it is important to maintain this level of discipline.

When you reach university, you may be tricked into thinking that first year doesn't count. This is an experiment and you are being tested to see if you will try and get away with as little work as possible. This is also the wrong mentality to adopt! Every year counts, because every year is a year that you should use to maximise yourself.

First year is the year that you should seek to create strong a foundation, as this will later act as a stepping stone. At this stage, it is important to note that not every single job for which you apply, will accept you. It is important to pick yourself back up and not get discouraged into thinking that it's pointless, especially if you have dedicated a lot of time to your job application.

A more optimistic way of dealing with rejection is to ask why you were rejected, if undisclosed in the rejection letter or email. In view of the reasons for the rejection, work on the areas identified as your weak points. Build your skill-set to such a degree that you are able to meet the criteria that every top employer wants to see in a potential employee.

As much as we all crave success, we need to also know that success comes with its own timing. During your time at uni, you need to realise this and make sure that you have the capacity and character to handle success when it does come.

'Success is one of the most expensive costs you will incur in life, but it is something that we can all afford'. Whilst you are in the process of maximising yourself at uni, you will begin to have a stronger understanding of your strengths and capabilities. In fact, you might even get inspired to enter into the world of self-employment through having a business idea.

Countless businesses have been started by uni students. A prime example of this is the world's largest social media outlet, started by the famous Mark Elliot Zuckerberg, who was a computer engineering student at the Harvard University. He launched a site that was meant to connect students at his university and, within a month, the network had spread over to other universities and now, of course, Facebook has over 845 million members worldwide.

Even closer to home is the story of Edwin Broni-Mensah, founder a social enterprise which aims to 'provide the gift of fresh water to everyone all over the world'. According to the Guardian newspaper, 'it was through playing squash at university that Broni-Mensah came up with the idea'.

Since its launch Give me Tap has won Mr Broni-Mensah an award for 'most outstanding black student in Britain'.

These are just a couple of examples of how students have maximised their potential. They may have come to uni with the view to enter into the working world, but during their journey, other opportunities arose. They took advantage of these chances and, as a result, left uni with a view to enter into the world of self-employment. There is nothing stopping you from being enterprising. The next successful person we could be reading about in the newspapers could be you.

Personal development

Prior to entering university, it is important that you write down your goals. Detail the things you would like to attain at the end of each academic year. You can stick this on your wall to constantly remind you of your focus.

As far as the academic side of things is concerned, it is important to enrol on to a course that you are passionate about, so that you are not just studying the course because you have nothing better to do. Make sure that you are studying it because it is an area of life that you would like to investigate and learn more about. If you can study and not feel like you are studying, you are on to a winner, as you will automatically find yourself doing more research on the subject, because of your passion. This is all basic stuff, but you will be surprised at how many people miss the mark in order to please those close to them. However discretion is advised, as some of today's universities offer what have been dubbed as 'Mickey-mouse degrees', that is, degrees without substance.

Upon arriving at uni, immediately you faced with the task of meeting a lot of new people during Fresher's weeks. This is an opportunity to find like-minded people. The company you keep is essential as people can either pull you up or pull you down. As soon as you know the date of your Fresher's fair, make sure that you create time to attend, as this will open many doors for you. Have a look around at the fair and find societies that give you the opportunity to develop your hobbies. For example, if you enjoy dancing in your spare time, make sure you join a dance society. This provides you with space to get away from studies and focus on something that you like.

Another important factor of Fresher's week would be to get into a society that allows you to gain or develop your leadership skills. To be the 'best of the best in life', you have to maintain the mind of a leader. If you are looking to work for someone else, it is wise to follow this up too. Employers these days are mostly interested in students that have had some sort of involvement in leadership.

Networking

It is becoming more apparent that the saying "It is not what you know, but who you know" is actually true. Sometimes you may find that your degree is not strong enough to link you to the perfect life-opportunity. In actual fact, it could be you meeting the right person that will help you. This is only possible when you place yourself in an environment that permits you to do so.

Networking events are the best opportunity for you to show employers that you have taken time outside university to pursue your career. It is an opportunity for you to sell yourself. It's like a cost-free interview, as you don't have to go through a long application process and - if you are lucky enough - a job opportunity could possibly come along with it.

It is also important to find someone that can give you one-on-one training in whatever you want to maximise yourself in, whether in your career, talent or faith. Look for someone who can mentor you. Let's not forget that we all live in a busy world, so if you are going to be mentored, make sure you make your mentor's time and effort not go to waste. Mentors are good, because they can help you with application forms and, most importantly, aid personal development and growth.

After putting all of the above into practice, you can be sure that you will be well on your way to becoming the crème-de-la crème of your university. Clean and polished for the top employers to recruit, while not forgetting that this can also come with its own timing. Alternatively, you could be working towards moving into your own field of business. As you begin on your road to success, don't forget to bring others with you as well.

The Grace matters more than the Grade

Although we have highlighted the practical steps of how one can become an outstanding student, grace is the most necessary and vital resource that will bring the fruit of these practical steps into reality. Drawing near to the closing stages of my final year, I have discovered that although I had embraced a positive mind-set and attitude toward working hard, it was not enough. I had to tap into the area of grace. I had to understand and realise that I could only work hard using the grace with which I had been provided. Once this grace had been removed, having a good mind-set and aptitude could only take me so far, and that wasn't far enough.

Never take the grace of God for granted; it is the very thing that enables you to read this very book. At times it may be hard to conceive, however tomorrow is not guaranteed, but given only through the grace of God. What I had to learn as individual is that it is not my hard work that has brought me this far, but it is simply the grace of God. I pray that the grace of God will continue to rest upon you as you read this book.

Testimonies

Hayley, BA Drama

It began in February 2011. I was in bed, thinking about my future after university. I became increasingly worried, because I felt my chosen degree limited me to a few options in terms of career. I therefore did extensive research into what opportunities were available for me in terms of gaining experience. However, through this research I discovered that most of the internships and courses were commenced during term time.

In addition to this, all the deadlines for the summer internships and courses had already passed. At this point I was on the verge of giving up, until I suddenly remembered a performance I was involved in during the Christmas holidays. Some of the actors I worked with in this show were part of a company called the National Youth Theatre.

I decided to audition for their annual two week course in the summer, which is very competitive. It was at the audition that I was informed that 4500 apply to audition and only 500 would get in. At this moment, I immediately called on God's help. I really wanted to be part of this amazing opportunity. I prayed before and after the audition, thanking God continuously.

I waited eight weeks for the results and it was during that time I began to doubt my ability as an actress, and my chances of getting onto the course. All of these anxieties clouded my hope of getting in and I became very pessimistic about the whole process.

Nevertheless, I continued to pray and trust that whatever the outcome, maybe it happened for a reason beyond my understanding. However, by the grace of God, I got accepted onto the two week National Youth Theatre course. This result was a reminder of the benefit of trusting and believing. It made me excited and intrigued as to what God had planned for me in my life and from this point on I vowed to have a closer relationship with God.

Looking back on this experience, I realised it couldn't be achieved by myself. I had to call on God, as he was the only one who could make these opportunities possible. This experience has also taught me trust like Abraham did in Genesis 15v 6 - 7.

PART 7

The Uni Experiment Explained

CHAPTER 19
Life after the Student Life

When you've completed your degree, the student life ends and life in the real world begins. Similar to when you initially go to uni, this too can be a daunting step especially as issues, including relocation, job hunting and financial pressure, come to bear. This transition is a crucial phase, as students become recognised as adult members of society.

Relocation

The first issue we are going to look at is whether to relocate or not. According to the UNITE report (2007), 'A third of students (29%) actually plan to settle in the university town/city once they complete their studies'. There may be a variety of reasons to either stay or go back home. In making this decision, seek advice from someone who has your best interests at heart. Most importantly, make sure that wherever you end up, God is involved in the decision.

Testimonies

Ayo, BSc Molecular Medicine and Biochemistry

Currently I'm still in Colchester, which makes me part of the 29% of students, which to be honest wasn't part of my original plan. Initially I planned to move to Norwich to go to the University of East Anglia, but having got into Anglia Ruskin University, I felt like God wanted me to stay in Colchester. It wasn't on my heart to move home, because I was mindful of possible confrontations at home, as I was now very independent. Therefore, in the interest of peace, I moved out of my mum's home.

Whilst I was at uni, I had several positions within the Christian society - Jesus Alive Fellowship (JAF). There, I was the Choir leader in my 2nd year and the Vice President in my 3rd year.

Staying in Colchester, I now attend Kesed Church. My experience here is truly an example of God testing and training me for further purposes. I'm in the worship team and am the Church's youth pastor. I found it funny that I was so busy asking God, "why me", to see where God was taking me, that it wasn't until I arrived at each new step that I understood his plan a little more. It makes me wonder, "what next?", but I'll leave it in his hands!

Dele, BSc Business Management

Being at home has been really tough. I'm even laughing as I write this. It's so different to uni, in that all the privacy I had as a student has basically gone. Especially in sharing a room with a sibling and having parents complain every minute.

I just have to thank God for family, because - even with all the negatives - there are many positives to being back at home, especially with my siblings. Being at uni for three years has meant that I haven't really been around for them, so it's good to be back at home and just be an older brother again.

Being at home and away from uni has also allowed me to focus more on the talents that God has given me and, just having more confidence, has let me come out of my shell and use those talents to bless other people. So, all I can say for now is watch this space.

Not having the comforts of the student life

The second issue to consider is handling life without the comforts of the student life. This is a weaning process, where we must learn to stand on our own two feet. Gone are the financial cushions provided by student finance or the safety of a readily accessible social network of friends. Thus, it is important to keep in touch with the friends you've made at uni, whether it's attending birthday and graduation parties, or - dare I say it - weddings.

Testimonies

Ayo, BSc Molecular Medicine and Biochemistry
Leaving the student life behind and moving on to the next step was daunting, but very exciting. One thing I can say about life now is that it definitely has been about the application of the life-lessons I learnt whilst I was at uni. Uni was where I 'grew up' and matured, but now it feels like God has been saying, 'prove it!'

After speaking to other friends who graduated in previous years, I realised that the Christian society I attended provided a structure and fellowship, which I wouldn't necessarily get outside of Uni. If I wasn't careful, it would have become a crutch that would soon cease to be available to me as I left uni.

The society was definitely a place where I had to develop my faith and therefore it complemented my relationship with God, but it didn't define the relationship. Being mindful of this definitely made my transition into the 'real world' a lot easier.

Dele, BSc Business Management

At first I thought it might be tough not being part of a campus fellowship. This was largely due to all the stories from previous graduates about how hard life after uni was, without the constant fellowship a Christian society provided.

But I haven't really felt like that. Not that I don't miss the fellowship. I thank God for the fellowship and the people who were in it, because it was essentially was a family of Christ-minded people, helping to pull each other up, in order to be more like Christ. So in that aspect, I miss having people there making sure you're alright and checking up on you and praying for you.

But do I miss it? No! Because leaving the fellowship doesn't mean that I've left the presence of God. He's continually watching over me, because He's with me every step of the way. Also being at home and going to Church, there are young adult groups which I have been involved with that are similar to the fellowship, making the transition from uni to home that much easier.

Tolu, BSc Biomedical Science

Initially I was slightly worried (ok, slightly is a big understatement), about the changes that would come after going back home from being an independent university student. A lot was going to change for me. For instance, the majority of the people with whom I had formed close friendships were either staying at uni or graduating with me. I knew things wouldn't be the same.

Prior to my university journey, I had a lot of responsibilities at home, so going to uni allowed me to spread my wings and breathe. But despite that, being back at home hasn't been as bad as I thought it would be and my independence hasn't been squashed, but supported.

A big challenge was learning to depend fully on God for everything, especially in the area of finance. Although I had got a job, it felt like God didn't want me to rely on it for provision, but on Him. This is something I believe I had to learn since I wasn't getting a constant supply of student loan anymore.

Leaving the campus fellowship didn't leave me feeling empty, contrary to common experiences. That being so, I really do miss being in a campus fellowship, growing together with people, seeing lives being transformed for Christ and having the constant encouragement, support and accountability! However, I have made sure to get myself involved in other Christian groups outside uni.

Financial pressures of life after the student life

The third issue to consider is the financial pressure of life after the student life. This can be a particularly trying period, especially if you fail to get immediate employment. It is common to blame parental control as the driving force behind the link between going back home and the loss of independence. Equally important, if not more, and slightly less obvious, is the lack of money as the driving force behind the link. Taking on less-qualified jobs, whilst in search for a graduate or a white-collar job, can work to your advantage as it brings in the necessary income which is key to your independence.

Testimonies

Jemma, BA Criminology with Social Psychology
Regardless of the financial struggles of the world, the redundancy of many, and the rising unemployment rates amongst graduates, I remembered the amazing promise written in Psalms 91v7.

After finishing uni, I had high goals and aspirations, very little money, and a lot to do. As well as being young, social pressures of events, birthdays, graduations, and post-university catch ups all required some sort of financial provision; provision I did not have.

Over the course of eight months, from my graduation in July to March the following year, I was jobless. I was quite happy, which came as a surprise to most, and often I found myself having to explain my decision to walk this path, but – also - during that time I received at lot of encouragement from the people around me.

I may have been financially broke, but I was spiritually well taken care of. I may not have been able to obtain my first car, or have the deposit ready for a flat, or have a brand new suit for interviews or a shiny new outfit for everyone's birthdays, but I tell you this: God always provided for me.

From gifts for friends, offering and tithes, to giving back to my Mom and Dad, I may have not been wealthy, but there was never a moment that I could not give, which still amazes me 'til this day, as I had no paid job. I continued to give, continued to follow the Lord strongly and stood proud that he had asked me to take on such a challenging walk of faith at that point in my life.

Job hunting

The final issue we are going to deal with is the process of job hunting. The experience of many graduates suggests that this can be a very tough process. It may take up to several months to even get an interview, let alone a decent job. At this stage, it is important to keep trusting that God has something planned for you. The blessings from the Daniel Experiment (Chapter 7) are not just for exams, but they echo right through to job interviews, as well as your performance in your career. You too can experience the great favour bestowed on Daniel and his three friends in Daniel 1v18-20.

Testimonies

Jemma, BA Criminology with Social Psychology

When I began the job hunting process, I quickly realised that degree doesn't equal job. I soon found myself having to consider taking absolutely any job going, simply because so many professionals had been made redundant in the recession and I was a small fish compared to them all. So it slowly became less of 'the dream' job hunt, and more of the 'I need to survive, give me any job going' job hunt.

During this period, a friend of mine challenged me to exercise my faith in applying for post-university jobs. I was then determined to start applying for jobs boldly, including jobs for which I felt under qualified. However, I felt like I would only be able to do so upon receiving guidance from God regarding applications and opportunities. I also knew that I wouldn't have to wait long, as I sensed that God was going to show me my next step.

True to form, God showed me my next step. He literally displayed it in front of me after I got off the train on way home from church. As I changed platforms and turned around, I realised I stood right in front of a great huge sign that read, 'we need you'. I hadn't laughed so hysterically in such a long time, but in pausing, I felt God telling me that this was it. Confused and giggling I wrote down the information just in time as the train pulled away off home.

I went home and prayed about it and felt the same way. I felt that God was calling me to this place. So I did some research and soon discovered that the job was actually in the financial sector. Growing up, I was never fond of maths, so going into the financial sector made me question whether this was really where God wanted me.

Remembering my friend's advice to exercise more faith, I applied anyway. To my surprise, I was invited along to go through the interview and screening and made it to the final stages of the selection process. The interview for this job has been the best in my life to date.

Unfortunately, in the end I wasn't able to get the job. I made a vital mistake of crossing out some work in my assessment test at the last minute and had no time to rewrite it as eloquently as planned. Candidates could not proceed with unanswered questions, so I didn't get the job. I felt discourage and soon fell into a slump of upset.

Not long after that, I reignited my commitment to staying strong in the Lord, and literally - soon after praying - I received a phone call. It was from the same organisation. They said that they had another position and asked if I was interested. I said yes, sure. The lady on the phone explained that she would email over some forms, so that they could start the screening and interviewing process. I said ok, but felt disappointed that I would have to go through the same process all over again. However, I felt better in praying, knowing that God wanted me in that organisation. It was just left for him to now put me in the right position.

A few hours later, the same lady called back, I hadn't even managed to fill in the forms yet. She asked again if I wanted the job, and I said yes definitely. She replied, "Ok, great, you start Monday 9 am; I've just emailed you the address and the details of your new manager." Astonished, I squeaked "Ok, thank you!" and immediately started thanking and praising God.

CHAPTER 20

Catalyst or Coincidence

The student life is a journey that is full of opportunities; opportunities to grow up or stay immature. It is a journey full of doors; some open and some closed - and thank God for the closed doors! At the end of the journey, we are left with memories, some more pleasant than others. These memories often define our time at uni.

This is all fairly obvious. However what is rather less obvious and, what a lot of students fail to realise, is that these opportunities or doors arise by design. In actual fact, they act as catalysts to speed up the development of your faith, character and intellect. This is contrary to the belief that coincidence is the reason behind the opportunities that are present in your life.

Experiments are full of catalysts;
Experiences are full of coincidences

The glass is either half full or half empty depending on your outlook on life. Similarly, the university journey is either an *experiment* or an *experience* depending on your outlook on the student life. By now, I hope that you are beginning to see the student life as an experiment and not merely an experience.

Viewing the student life as an experiment leads to the view that every situation that you will face as a student has been designed with you in mind. In 1 Corinthians 10v13 we read that, 'The temptations in your life are no different from what others experience. And God is faithful. He will not allow the temptation to be more than you can stand.' Every issue, opportunity or door that comes your way at uni has been filtered through the hand of God.

Knowing that you are under the experiment can work to your advantage, in so many ways. One way is that we know that, whenever an experiment is being conducted, there is always an end goal. Namely, it's not without purpose. This can be a very comforting realisation during trying periods. You can be confident that, under the experiment, there is no pain without purpose.

In Romans 8v18 Paul writes, 'Yet what we suffer now is nothing to be compared to the glory He will reveal to us later'. To a lesser extent, the sleepless nights, the setbacks, and challenges of being a Christian student, are nothing to be compared to the glory of graduation day, to play on the above verse.

Viewing the student life as merely an experience leads to the view that 'things just happen at uni'. After all, experiences are full of coincidences. By adopting this view, you may miss the opportunities, the people, and the blessings that God may be bringing into your life. This is because it is easy to dismiss these things as mere coincidences.

To illustrate this, my final year exams provided me with the opportunity to either view the whole process as a catalyst or dismiss it as a mere coincidence and thus rob myself and others of the crucial lesson God was trying to teach me. During the revision period, I had it in my mind that my first and last exams would be much easier than all the exams in the middle. Having previously taken a re-sit, there was one particular module

I feared the most. Funnily enough, the re-sit came a short while after writing the eBook 'How to get a first and avoid a resit; God's way'. Accidental or by design; you be the judge.

It turns out that I ended up doing a lot worse in the exams I thought would be much easier. Whereas, I did really well in the exams I thought would be much tougher, including the module I feared the most. It is easy to dismiss it as a mere coincidence. Common sentiments may include, 'It just so happened that things turned out that way', or 'He probably worked a bit harder for the harder modules'. There is an element of truth in the second sentiment; however there is also a risk of overlooking the lesson that God wants us to learn.

You are probably wondering what I learnt from this experiment. I learnt that God really does have His hand over everything. There is nothing that comes our way that has not been filtered through the hand of God.

I learnt to trust God with my exams. In Isaiah 40v4a (NIV) we learn that this same God said, 'every valley shall be raised up, every mountain and hill made low'. In the same way He made what was 'easy' for me, 'hard' and what was hard, He made it easy. In doing this He gets all the glory. It is appropriate at this stage to say that, if it wasn't for God, I wouldn't have graduated, let alone graduated with a 1st class degree. There is nothing to stop God from doing the same for you, so long as you glorify Him for it.

What Aspects of the student life have you found to be an experiment?

Testimonies

Tolu, BSc Biomedical Science

Honestly if there is one thing I can say about my experience at university, it is that I left a totally different person to how I arrived. I came in with a lot of baggage; many issues that I thought could never go away. I remember in my last year of sixth form, I prayed constantly that God would keep me and I wouldn't go off the rails. Looking back over the last 3 years I'm so grateful that He honoured those two simple prayers.

Now I won't lie and say I was a goody two shoes, in fact even after praying those prayers I knew in my heart that I wanted to do my own thing and have fun. But He still brought me back to Him. There was a big improvement in my spiritual life at university (now, thinking about it, probably one of the last places you think that would happen - but it did!). God did this through the campus fellowship that I attended, where I met other Christians who were on fire for God and loving it!

It was inspiring and encouraging. It was wonderful to meet so many people in Christ from different walks of life. It was like having a family on campus. I'm not trying to paint a perfect picture here because like any family issues did arise (which did eventually get sorted out!).

The times where I felt I was being tested at university were most definitely in some of my interactions with people. In other words, there were times my patience had been seriously tested in dealing with people. I would say scientists put me in a quite a few tricky situations, especially because I was learning (and still learning) how to handle situations in a Christ-like manner. I think something I really learnt from those situations was that, in life, you are going to meet so many different people with different ways of thinking, backgrounds and life experiences and that I wasn't to try and change people to suit me, but to accept them and learn to overlook their short-comings the same way God does for me.

Another "experiment" I would say I was put in was at the end of my second year when I had received my result for the year. I can honestly say I was being tested. I felt I had worked hard and had nothing to show for it. After getting over the disappointment, I took the uni's offer to retake an exam, but still my grade didn't change because of my performance in the exam. At this point, it affected me so much that I was ready to leave university and give up on education as a whole. Thankfully God picked me up, really empowered me to carry on and saw me through to the end of university.

Dele, BSc Business Management

I felt that the whole experience of uni was an experiment, in the sense that being a Christian at university had its own trials and temptations. To be honest, just the whole walk with Christ being tested every day at university was tough.

I thank God for carrying me through and making my relationship with Him that much stronger and for me not leaving university the same way I entered. Everyone who knows me knows that a scripture which I held close to me whilst at university was James 4v4. This allowed me to better prepare for the temptations that came along my way. That, as well as my brothers and sisters from the Christian society who were always there for me and each other, making sure that, if we did fall, we would pick each other back up.

Ayo, BSc Molecular Medicine and Biochemistry

As I reflect on life now, I really see that God has made a declaration over me. Him pulling me through various tests is proof of his unfailing love for me. Just like scientific experiments (just read my dissertation!), I don't always go perfectly to plan, but that doesn't mean the declaration can't be proved; it just may mean that I take a little bit longer than my creator wanted.

He has invested His effort, love and patience into my life so that I may be a living testimony to the world, just as a publication provides proof of a scientist's theory. If I could remind people of anything, it's that - as uni comes to an end - it's easy to think, "wow I've come so far". For most people, that's probably true. But remember, God is planning to take you much further. Uni is only the training ground, so make sure you're ready for the main event.

Observation

Review of the chapters

The social scientists have come to the end of their covert experiments. The students at Laban's Court 13.1 have endured countless tests and trails without knowing it. These were designed to understand the university experience, and to find evidence to disprove the view that a degree was losing its value.

In the end, the scientists concluded that even though the degree was losing its value, going to university was more than about obtaining a degree. From the various observations they carried out, the scientists discovered that university aided students in becoming adults. The university journey gave students, a chance to discover themselves and what they stood for, especially amongst followers of Christ.

For the most part, the scientists chose not to directly intervene or speed up the process in conducting the experiments. It was hoped that in the fullness of time, their hypotheses would either be confirmed or rejected. There were occasions where the scientists used catalysts to speed up an experiment, as is common practice among scientists.

In particular, the A2 sheet of paper with information about the student's likes and dislikes helped the scientists to design the experiments with the students in mind. In view of this, the scientists sent out a popular Christian text message to one of the students, ending with "If you aren't ashamed to do this, please pass this on. Jesus said, if you are ashamed of me, I will be ashamed of you before my Father". This helped to speed up the process of testing whether a student would choose to hide his or her faith or not.

Whilst the scientists were there to test their hypotheses through the use of experiments, they unintentionally achieved an even greater feat than that. By introducing catalysts at various points, it meant that the students under the experiments faced a lot more pressure than their peers. Being tried and tested in this way meant that the students who endured came out of the experiments more mature and successful than would been the case, in the absence of such catalysts.

Experiment

Bias the experiments to your advantage! If you know that you are under an experiment, the results are mostly likely going to be biased. With this in mind, why not bias them to your advantage. For example, being aware of the potential causes of dropout rates will bias the outcome to your advantage, as you are more likely to avoid the causes that lead to dropping out of university.

Appendix A

Dominant Quality League Table

Times Rank 2012	Institution	Dominant Quality ranking	
1	Oxford	Outstanding	
2	Cambridge	Outstanding	
3	London School of Economics	Outstanding	
4	Imperial College	Outstanding	
5	University College London	Outstanding	
6	Durham	Outstanding	
6	St Andrews	Outstanding	
8	Warwick	Outstanding	
9	Lancaster	Outstanding	
10	Exeter	Outstanding	
11	York	Outstanding	Outstanding
12	Bath	Outstanding	
13	Bristol	Outstanding	
14	Sussex*	Above average	
15	Edinburgh	Outstanding	
16	Nottingham	Outstanding	
17	Sheffield	Outstanding	
17	Leicester	Outstanding/above average	
19	Southampton	Outstanding	
20	Loughborough*	Above average	
21	Buckingham*	Average	
22	Glasgow	Outstanding	
23	School of Oriental and African Studies	Outstanding/above average	
24	King's College London*	Outstanding	
25	Newcastle*	Outstanding	
26	Birmingham	Outstanding/above average	Above Average
27	East Anglia	Above average	
28	Royal Holloway	Above average	
29	Surrey	Above average	

Times Rank 2012	Institution	Dominant Quality ranking
30	Leeds	Above average
31	Liverpool	Above average
32	Manchester	Outstanding/above average
33	Reading	Above average
34	Strathclyde	Above average
35	Cardiff	Above average
36	Aston	Above average/average
37	Queen Mary, London	Above average
38	Queen's Belfast	Above average
39	Kent	Above average/average
40	Dundee	Above average
41	Essex	Above average/average
42	Aberdeen	Above average
43	Aberystwyth*	Average
44	Heriot-Watt	Above average
45	Keele	Average
46	Stirling	Average
47	City	Above average/average
48	Oxford Brookes	Above average/average
49	Swansea	Above average/average
50	Goldsmiths College	Below average
51	Brunel*	Above average
52	Robert Gordon	Average
53	Hull	Average
54	Chichester	Below average
55	Lincoln	Average/Below average
56	Ulster	Average/Above average
57	Bangor*	Below average
58	Plymouth	Average
59	Huddersfield	Below average
60	Northumbria*	Below average
61	Central Lancashire*	Below average
62	Bradford	Average/Below average
62	Bournemouth	Average
64	Hertfordshire	Average/Below average
65	Gloucestershire	Average/Below average
66	Nottingham Trent	Average/Below average

Average

APPENDIX A

Times Rank 2012	Institution	Dominant Quality ranking		
67	West of England	Average/Below average		
67	Portsmouth	Average/Below average		
69	Brighton	Average/Below average		
69	Winchester	Average/Below average		
71	Edinburgh Napier	Average/Below average		
71	Chester	Below average/poor		
71	Sheffield Hallam	Average/Below average		
71	UWIC, Cardiff	Below average		
75	Glasgow Caledonian	Below average		
76	Coventry	Below average		
77	Edge Hill*	Poor		
78	Queen Margaret Edinburgh	Below average		
79	Roehampton	Average/Below average		
80	Teesside	Below average/poor		Below Average
80	Sunderland*	Poor		
82	Cumbria	Below average		
82	University of the Arts, London	Below average		
84	Bath Spa	Below average		
85	De Montfort*	Poor		
86	York St John	Below average/poor		
87	Birmingham City*	Poor		
88	Canterbury Christ Church	Below average		
89	Staffordshire*	Poor		
90	Trinity St Davids	Below average/poor		
91	Salford	Average/Below average		
92	Northampton	Poor		
93	Glamorgan	Below average/poor		
94	Worcester	Below average/poor		
94	Middlesex	Poor		
96	Westminster*	Average/Below average		
97	Kingston	Below/poor		
98	Manchester Metropolitan	Below average		Poor
99	Greenwich	Poor		
100	Liverpool John Moores	Below average/poor		
101	Abertay	Below average/poor		
102	Glyndŵr	Poor		
102	University for Creative Arts	Below average		

Times Rank 2012	Institution	Dominant Quality ranking
104	Leeds Metropolitan	Below average/poor
104	UWCN, Newport	Poor
106	Bedfordshire	Poor
107	Derby	Poor
108	Anglia Ruskin	Below average/poor
109	Southampton Solent	poor
110	Buckinghamshire New	Poor
111	Highlands and Islands	Poor
112	West of Scotland	Below average/Poor
113	London South Bank	Poor
114	Bolton	Poor
115	East London	Poor
116	London Metropolitan	Poor

Appendix B

Institution Grouping

Russell Group
University of Birmingham
University of Bristol
University of Cambridge
Cardiff University
University of Edinburgh
University of Glasgow
Imperial College London
King's College London
University of Leeds
University of Liverpool
London School of Economics
University of Manchester
University of Newcastle-upon-Tyne
University of Nottingham
University of Oxford
Queen's University Belfast
University of Sheffield
University of Southampton
University College London
University of Warwick

1994 GROUP
University of Bath
Birkbeck, University of London
Durham University
University of East Anglia
University of Essex
University of Exeter
Goldsmiths College

1994 GROUP

Institute of Education
Royal Holloway and Bedford New College
University of Lancaster
University of Leicester
Loughborough University
Queen Mary and Wesfield College
University of Reading
University of St Andrews
School of Oriental and African Studies
University of Surrey
University of Sussex
University of York

UNIVERSITY ALLIANCE

Aberystwyth University
Bournemouth University
University of Bradford
Cardiff Met University
De Montfort University
University of Glamorgan
Glasgow Cal University
University of Hertfordshire
University of Huddersfield
University of Lincoln
Liverpool John Moorse
Manchester Met University
University of Northumbria at Newcastle
Nottingham Trent University
Open University
Oxford Brookes University
University of Plymouth
University of Portsmouth
University of Salford
Sheffield Hallam University
Teesside University
University of Wales, Newport
University of West of England

MILLION PLUS
University of Abertay Dundee
Anglia Ruskin University
Bath Spa University
University of Bedfordshire
Birmingham City University
University of Bolton
Buckinghamshire New University
University of Central Lancashire
Coventry University
University of Derby
University of East London
Edinburgh Napier University
University of Greenwich
Kingston University
Leeds Met University
London Met University
London South Bank University
Middlesex University
University of Northampton
Roehampton University
Southampton Solent
Staffordshire University
University of Sunderland
University of West London
University of the West of Scotland
University of Wolverhampton

Endnotes

User Guide
Introduction to psychology p212, Publication can be found at
http://www.blackwellpublishing.com/intropsych/pdf/chapter10.pdf

Chapter 2
http://www.guardian.co.uk/society/joepublic/2008/sep/09/freshers.week.binge.drinking
http://www.cueproject.org.uk/findings/

Chapter 3
UNITE Student Experience report 2007
Draper, S.W. (2006, July 12) *Tinto's model of student retention*
http://www.psy.gla.ac.uk/~steve/localed/tinto.html (visited 2012 June)

Chapter 4
http://www.unite-group.co.uk/press-centre/press-releases/university-life-a-head-start-by-any-degree.go

Chapter 7
http://daniel-fast.com/index.html

Chapter 8
http://www.guardian.co.uk/education/2011/aug/18/freshers-week-questions-university
Yip, A. K. T., Keenan, M. and Page, S. (2011) *Religion, Youth and Sexuality: Selected Key Findings from a Multi-faith Exploration.* Nottingham: University of Nottingham.

Chapter 9
Gay-Lynn Taylor (summer 2009), 'too busy for God?', 'the student & young lawyers' journal of the lawyers' Christian fellowship' pp 20 – 22'
http://www.cgministries.co.uk/blog/?page_id=6&paged=3

Chapter 10
http://www.cliffcollege.ac.uk/page/certificate_in_christian_mentoring_and_coaching
http://www.itsgoodtotalk.org.uk/
http://www.acc-uk.org/

Chapter 11
Economics by Mr John Sloman and Prof Alison Wride (Paperback - 23 Jul 2009)

Chapter 13
http://www.unite-group.co.uk/press-centre/press-releases/university-life-a-head-start-by-any-degree.go
http://www.startmarriageright.com/2011/05/ring-by-spring/
http://news.bbc.co.uk/1/hi/health/801872.stm

Chapter 14
http://www.halifax.co.uk/bankaccounts/pdf/student-current-account-guide.pdf
http://www.santander.co.uk/
http://www.lloydstsb.com/current_accounts/Student_account.asp
http://www.natwest.com
http://www.hsbc.co.uk/1/2/current-accounts/student-bank-account/details
http://www.hsbc.co.uk/1/2/current-accounts/student-bank-account/bursary
http://www.barclays.co.uk/Otheraccounts/Studentaccounts
www.family-action.org.uk
Factsonfees.com

Frequently asked questions about student finance from September 2012; Department for Business, Innovation and Skills. Publication available on *www.bis.gov.uk*

Chapter 15

http://www.guardian.co.uk/money/2011/aug/12/student-debt-to-rocket-2012-freshers
http://www.direct.gov.uk/en/moneytaxandbenefits/benefitstaxcreditsandothersuppo rt/illorinjured/dg_10018978
www.16-25railcard.co.uk
Saynoto0870.com
Billmonitor.com
Resourcefulcook.com

Chapter 16

Measuring what counts or counting what can be measure? HEFCE report 2008
Unite Student Experience Report 2007

Chapter 17

Higher Education Statistics Agency HESA *www.HESA.org.uk*
Becker. Gary S, (1962) Investment in Human Capital: A Theoretical Analysis
Investopedia http://www.investopedia.com/terms/r/rational-choice-theory.asp#axzz1yEuEJims
Draper, S.W. (2006, July 12) *Tinto's model of student retention http://www.psy.gla.ac.uk/~steve/localed/tinto.html* (visited 2012 June)

Chapter 18

http://www.inspiringinterns.com/blog/2012/04/8-successful-student-businesses-started-at-university/
http://www.guardian.co.uk/business/2011/mar/06/young-british-entrepreneurs

Chapter 19
Unite Student Experience Report 2007

Chapter 20
http://www.lulu.com/shop/tino-zishiri/how-to-get-a-first-or-avoid-a-resit-gods-way/ebook/product-20254271.html

Printed in Great Britain
by Amazon